THE SAFE ZONE

A KID'S GUIDE TO PERSONAL SAFETY

THE SAFE ZONE

A KID'S GUIDE TO PERSONAL SAFETY

by Donna Chaiet and Francine Russell

photographs by Lillian Gee

MORROW JUNIOR BOOKS
NEW YORK

I'd like to thank my husband, George Tovar, and my mother, Ann Russell, for their invaluable comments, suggestions, and critiques. I would also like to thank the students of Ms. Croft's and Ms. Silverman's fifth-grade classes at Grant Elementary in Santa Monica, California; they offered great insight into what it's like being a kid in today's world.

Also, my thanks to God, who had to endure my many grumblings and complaints and pleas for help in the writing of this book. He listened patiently, then provided guidance, wisdom, inspiration, and the occasional miracle. May this book help in the battle for a safer world for all His children.

—Francine Russell

This is dedicated to Karen Chasen, my business partner (and sister!), who tirelessly edited and proofread this book. Many thanks to the parents and educators who engage Prepare and IMPACT Personal Safety to teach our programs to them and their children. Children's safety education is not a luxury; it is a necessity.

—Donna Chaiet

Text copyright © 1998 by Donna Chaiet and Francine Russell
Photographs copyright © 1998 by Lillian Gee

Published by Morrow Junior Books
a division of William Morrow and Company, Inc.
1350 Avenue of the Americas, New York, NY 10019
www.williammorrow.com

Printed in the United States of America.

10 9 8 7 6 5 4 3 2 1

Library of Congress Cataloging-in-Publication Data
Chaiet, Donna.
The safe zone: a kid's guide to personal safety/by Donna Chaiet and Francine Russell.
p. cm.
Summary: Discusses various self-defense options which may be used when in an
uncomfortable or unsafe situation and suggests what solutions might work in real life.
ISBN 0-688-15307-0
1. Safety education—Juvenile literature.   2. Children and strangers—Juvenile literature.
3. Child abuse—Prevention—Juvenile literature.   [1. Safety.   2. Strangers.   3. Child abuse.]
I. Russell, Francine.   II. Title.   HQ770.7.C48 1998   613.6'083—dc21   97-36309   CIP AC

Contents

INTRODUCTION   9

1 THE BASICS   11
What If...?   12
Awareness   13
Listen to Your Gut   17
Body Language   20
Use Your Voice   21
Self-Esteem   23
Build More Self-Esteem   24
Answers to "What If...?"   27

2 SETTING BOUNDARIES   30
What If...?   30
What Is a Boundary?   31
Physical Boundaries   31
How to Set a Physical Boundary   37
Feelings Boundaries   42
What If You Set a Boundary and People Still Don't Do What You Ask?   46
Answers to "What If...?"   47

3 MY BODY IS MINE   50
What If...?   50
What Is Unwanted Touch?   50
Stopping Unwanted Touch   51
Unwanted Touch from Other Kids   54
Unwanted Touch from Adults   56
Unwanted Touch from Strangers   60
Answers to "What If...?"   62

4 BULLIES   65
What If...?   65
Why Are Some People Bullies?   66
How to Avoid a Bully   68
How to Deal with a Bully   68
Answers to "What If...?"   80

5 STAYING SAFE AT HOME   84
What If...?   84
Pay Attention to Your Home Environment   85
How to Deal with Strangers at the Door   86
If Someone Tries to Get into Your Home   90
Dealing with Strangers on the Phone   92
Safety on the Internet   93
Answers to "What If...?"   96

6 SAFETY AWAY FROM HOME   98
What If...?   98
Target Denial   99
Be Aware   99
Plan Ahead   100
Listen to Your Gut   100
Use Your Voice   101
Safety in Your Car   107
Safety at School   108
Safety on Public Transportation   110
What If You're Lost?   112
A Word (or Two) About Alcohol and Drugs   113
Answers to "What If...?"   114

7 GETTING HELP   116
What If...?   116
We All Need Help Sometimes   117
Getting Help with Unwanted Touch   120

Answers to "What If...?"   125

8 STRANGERS   128
What If...?   128
How to Identify a Stranger   129
Four Key Safety Rules   129
Answers to "What If...?"   139

9 FIGHTING BACK   141
How to Recognize When You Need to Fight   142
One Last Chance...   142
Optimizing Your Size   143
Achieving Your Goal   144
    Target Areas   144
    Natural Weapons   144
    Fighting Spirit   147
What If There Is a Weapon Involved?   150

CONCLUSION   152

About Prepare and IMPACT Personal Safety   154
Getting Help   155
Other Books You May Want to Read   160

INTRODUCTION

Many people believe that self-defense means fighting. But the best self-defense has nothing to do with hitting, kicking, or punching. Self-defense has to do with being aware of your surroundings and being able to communicate with someone who may seem threatening. It sounds pretty basic, but these skills can actually help you avoid a physical attack. Sometimes, in very rare circumstances, physical fighting is necessary. But whenever you decide to fight with someone else, you risk getting hurt, even if you win. So fighting should always be the last thing you choose to do.

In this book we show you many different self-defense options. You will read about kids who find themselves in uncomfortable or unsafe situations—from confrontations with bullies in the school-yard to the threat of strangers outside the mall—and then see what solutions might work in real life.

But a book can't do everything. You can't just flip through these pages and hope to become a self-defense expert or a black belt in karate. This book is a guide. In order for it to help you, you have to *do* what it teaches.

There are things that you can do now to prepare yourself should you ever be in danger. Would you wait until your house was on fire to decide how to get out? Of course not. You'd decide ahead of time what your escape routes would be. The same is true for self-defense. It's hard to make decisions during an emergency, when you're scared and not thinking clearly. That's why it's important to practice the skills in this book and plan ahead for your safety.

As you get older, you cannot always depend on your parents or friends or teachers to come to your rescue. At some point in your life you may have to rely on yourself. And even though you may think that there's nothing you could do if you were alone and someone tried to hurt you, there are ways to avoid being a victim. So start learning *now* how to protect and defend yourself.

THE BASICS

1

Self-defense is made up of four key elements:

- **AWARENESS:** Where are you? Who is nearby? What's going on around you? Do you feel safe or does something feel wrong here?
- **BODY LANGUAGE:** What message do others get by the way you walk or the way you move or the way you deal with other people? Do you look like an easy target?
- **SELF-ESTEEM:** How do you feel about yourself? Do you believe you're worth defending? Do your feelings about yourself come through in your body language?
- **BOUNDARIES:** How do you let others know where you "draw the line"? What can you do if they don't listen?

We'll talk about these concepts in the next two chapters and show you ways to use them in different situations.

What if . . . you're walking home from school and you see an older boy coming toward you on the sidewalk. He's still a good distance away, but he has both hands in his pockets, and he's staring at you. You get a funny feeling in your stomach. It's daylight, there are cars passing by, and there are a couple of adults talking across the street. What do you do?

What if . . . you're really late for soccer practice. It's faster to cut through the alleyway behind your building than to go around the block. But sometimes there are high school kids hanging around there, drinking and smoking. What do you do?

What if . . . you and a friend are waiting for your mom to pick you up just outside the movie theater. You notice a man standing nearby who's wearing a long overcoat even though it's not that cold and it's not raining. You have the feeling he's watching you, but he glances away whenever you look in his direction. What do you do?

AWARENESS

Awareness means noticing who and what is around you. Where is the nearest safe place? Your home, your car, a public place with other people, a police station, a school or store with a security guard? How close is that stranger? Is he or she coming toward you? Can you get away from that person quickly by crossing the street, entering a store, or turning around and going the other way?

When you were younger, your parents or other caretakers looked out for you. They kept an eye on strangers and helped you avoid dangers. Now it's time for you to learn how to be aware and how to protect yourself when you're alone. Being aware is one of the easiest things you can do to stay safe.

Stand up, letting your arms hang down by your side. Stare straight ahead at a spot on the wall. Lift your arms straight up in front of you, away from your body, to shoulder level. Now wiggle your fingers, and slowly move your arms out toward your sides, keeping them at shoulder level. Keep looking at that wall in front of you. Stop when you reach the point where you can just barely see those wiggling fingers out of the corners of your eyes. This is what we call peripheral vision—what you can see out of the corners of your eyes.

Now put your hands down, and look straight ahead. Use your peripheral vision and notice what you can see. Turn your head from side to side and see how much more you can include in your sight. You can see nearly all the way around you when you use your peripheral vision and also turn your head from side to side. This is an excellent way to note your surroundings. The more you can see, the more aware you are.

You can use your peripheral vision to keep an eye on someone without looking directly at him or her. Whenever people pass you on a sidewalk or in a hall, turn your head to the side to watch them until they are quite far away from you, without turning completely around and staring at them.

Here are some questions to ask yourself to increase your awareness. Practice asking yourself these questions, even in situations where you feel safe:

- Are you someplace dark or well lit? Are there bushes, alleys, or vehicles where someone could hide? Are there other people around?
- How many people can you see? How close are they to you?
- What are they doing? Are they drunk, angry, laughing, or talking?
- Are they paying any attention to you?
- How do you feel about these people? Do you feel comfortable, safe, uneasy, threatened, or scared?
- What is around you? Do you see a security guard nearby? Is there somewhere safe that you can go to if you need to run? If you yell, are there others nearby who will hear you?

● What do you have with you: a backpack, a purse, a bicycle, a skateboard, books, groceries? What are you going to do with these things if you have to run away quickly? Be prepared to leave them behind if necessary.

> Take a walk down the block where you live. Ask your-self as many of the questions listed on the previous page as you can. As soon as you're back inside your house, write down everything you can remember about all the things you noticed. Do this once a week, and see if you can make your list longer and more complete each time. Notice what is always the same and what is different. You can also try this exercise in other places that are familiar to you, like right outside your school or in a relative's home, for more practice.

You can try out your awareness skills everywhere you go. At first you may feel strange, even a little paranoid. But you'll find that awareness gets easier with practice, and it will actually help lessen your fears because you'll feel more in control.

Being aware means using your common sense to avoid places that look dangerous or places that you know are dangerous. Don't take a shortcut or go exploring some new place if it means that you will be alone and far from help. Empty lots, vacant athletic fields, and high-crime neighborhoods are the types of places you want to avoid.

Choose to play or walk in areas where other people are close by. Travel with a friend or a group whenever possible. Stay in areas

no one else in the bathroom. Jenna went into one of the empty stalls.

Suddenly she had a strange feeling in the pit of her stomach. She slowly looked under the partition between the two stalls and saw very large cowboy boots—much too large to belong to a woman. There was a man in the next stall! Jenna quickly fixed her clothes and ran out of her stall. She stayed as far away from the middle stall as possible but kept her eyes on it until she reached the bathroom door.

She hurried back to her family and told them what had happened. Her parents went to the restaurant manager and explained the situation to him. He promised to alert security. Now that it was all over, Jenna started to shake. Her mother assured her that her trembling was just her body's way of reacting to something scary. She hugged Jenna and told her she had done the right thing by being aware and leaving the bathroom as soon as possible.

It is amazing how that feeling in your gut can warn you of possible danger. Sometimes it can seem like magic. Jenna wasn't even sure why she had a bad feeling, but she did the smart thing and listened to it. When she discovered where the bad feeling was coming from—the person in the next stall—she quickly got out of the bathroom.

Jenna's shakiness afterward is very common. When you're scared, your body releases a hormone called adrenaline. Have you ever been surprised by a loud noise? Remember how your that are well lit. Keep a lot of distance between you and p cars, especially vans.

Be aware when approaching groups of people that you d know. Turn around and leave if you sense any danger, using y peripheral vision to keep an eye on them.

LISTEN TO YOUR GUT

Have you ever had a bad feeling about something? You couldn't explain it in words maybe, but you just knew something was wrong? Maybe the hair on the back of your neck stood up, or you got a tingling sensation all over your body. Or maybe you felt as if there were a big knot in your stomach.

Often, when something is wrong, you get a feeling about it. We call this listening to your gut. It's an important warning signal. Many times our instincts know we're in danger before our minds do. When you get a bad feeling about a place or a person, don't ignore it. Leave the place; get away from that person; do whatever you have to do to be safe.

The following is based on a true story:

Trust Your Instincts and Leave
Jenna's aunt and uncle were in town for a convention and stay-ing at a nearby hotel. Jenna and her family met them for dinner in the hotel restaurant. While waiting for dessert, Jenna excused herself to go to the women's room. There were three stalls in the bathroom, and the middle one was occupied. There was

heart started beating hard? If you were sound asleep when the noise surprised you, you might suddenly find yourself sitting up, wide awake. This is what happens when your adrenaline starts working.

Adrenaline is a good thing. It sends extra blood to your heart and lungs. Your muscles tense, and you become very alert. This is called the fight or flight response. It means that your body is getting ready either to fight or to run away.

There are many types of situations that can cause your adrenaline to start pumping. You may feel it when someone sneaks up behind you and scares you. You will definitely feel it when walking through a haunted house at Halloween or exploring a strange place. Natural disasters—hurricanes, tornadoes, earthquakes—will cause it. You'll feel it if you are in an accident and someone gets hurt, and you'll feel it even if you only witness the accident. Getting a bad feeling in your gut will give you an adrenaline "rush," too.

Sometimes, when your adrenaline starts pumping, it can cause you to freeze. Have you ever been scared and found yourself frozen in one spot? You couldn't breathe or move. There is a good reason for this freeze response. It makes you pause and size up the situation, so you can decide what you should do. But you don't want to get stuck in the freeze response. To break it, take a deep breath, then let it out. You can also yell (we talk more about that in Chapter Two); it will get you breathing and moving fast!

Once the danger has passed, your knees may feel weak and you may feel shaky all over. This is normal. Your body is relaxing from its tense state during the adrenaline rush. If the crisis lasted a long time, as it might during a storm, you may feel sleepy afterward. That's also normal; your body needs to rest after all the excitement.

It can be scary when you get that feeling in your gut. It can be scary when you feel your adrenaline start pumping. But remember that both these things are good. They're your body's way of warning you of danger and helping you deal with it. Listening to your body's warning signals is a very good way to stay safe.

BODY LANGUAGE

Your body not only tells you certain things but also sends a message about you to the rest of the world. The way you walk, the way you sit, and your facial expressions all are part of your body language. Your body language expresses how you feel about yourself.

An assailant (someone who attacks another person) is looking

for a victim. He or she doesn't want trouble; he or she wants an easy target. In one study a number of prison inmates were shown a videotape of people walking down the street. The inmates were asked to pick which people they would choose as victims. The prisoners often chose the same people as targets on the basis of the body language of those people.

If you had been in that videotape, would you have been chosen as a target? Do you look at the ground when you walk? Do you avoid looking people in the eye? Do you seem timid and afraid? Do you bury your head in a book or turn the music up loud on your headphones so you can't hear anything else?

Target denial is a term that is used a lot in self-defense and in many martial arts. If you are sparring, you move out of the way so that your opponent's "target" is no longer where he thought it would be. You've denied him his target.

Similarly, you can deny an assailant his target simply by being aware and looking as if you were paying attention to your surroundings. Walk with your head up. Look around; notice everybody and everything around you. If you feel threatened, take action. Go to a safe place. Don't be an easy target.

USE YOUR VOICE

Your voice and the way you speak to someone are important parts of self-defense. If you feel threatened, you can use your voice to speak loudly and draw attention to yourself. Assailants don't want trouble, so if you start attracting a crowd, they're likely to leave.

Yelling for help can scare off an attacker. Yelling can also help break the freeze response, so your body starts breathing and moving again.

Stand with your feet slightly apart, your arms down by your sides. Place one hand on your stomach. Take a deep breath, and feel your stomach get bigger. Tighten your stomach to force the breath out. Do this a couple of times.

Now take another deep breath, but this time, as you tighten your stomach and exhale, yell *"No"* as loudly as you can. That's pretty loud, isn't it?

Practice yelling *"No"* a few times. This is the kind of yell you want to use in an emergency: strong, loud, and forceful. You can yell *"No"* or *"Help"* or *"Leave me alone"* or *"Go away"* or *"Back off."* If someone is trying to harm you and he or she hears this kind of yell coming out of you, he or she will probably think twice about attacking you. Your assailant may even change his or her mind and run away.

You can also use your voice to talk to other people and tell them how you feel. If a friend or family member hurts your feelings, you may need to tell him or her so. You can use your voice to seek help or advice. If you're being bullied or if someone has been hurting you, you can ask a friend or a trusted adult for help.

We don't often think of talking as a means of self-defense, but you will find in the following chapters that using your voice can be a powerful weapon.

SELF-ESTEEM

You've probably heard the term *self-esteem* before, but what does it mean? And what does it have to do with self-defense?

Self-esteem means "feeling good about yourself." It doesn't mean you're conceited or selfish. It means that you have confidence in yourself. You know that your feelings should be respected. You know that your life is worth defending.

We all have things about ourselves that we like and things that we wish we could change. We're all good at some things and not so great at others. Self-esteem means accepting our strengths and weaknesses and knowing that these are the things that make us special.

If people have low self-esteem, they may think that others are better or more important than they are. They may not think they're worth much. People with low self-esteem may look at the ground when they walk. Perhaps they speak very softly and avoid looking directly at others. Their body language gives off the message that they're scared and probably won't defend themselves. Remember, assailants are looking for easy targets. A person with low self-esteem looks like an easy target.

Having self-esteem gives you confidence. That confidence will show in your body language and in your voice. When you're confident, you will walk with your head up, making it easier to be more aware. When you're confident, you can look people in the eye and talk to them in a clear, strong voice. Your body language makes you look like the kind of person an assailant wants to avoid.

BUILD MORE SELF-ESTEEM

How do you increase your self-esteem? Here's an exercise for you to try:

> Make a list of all the things you do well. Include all your good qualities and things about yourself that you're proud of. Leave the list where you can readily find it, like inside your knapsack. When you're feeling low or discouraged, this list will help boost your self-esteem.

Here are a few more ideas for building self-esteem. See if you can think of any others.

● Choose friends who support and encourage you. Don't forget to return the favor to your friends by supporting and encouraging them.

● Avoid people who only criticize or put you down.

● Challenge yourself by learning new things. You might try painting. Or Rollerblading. Join a club. Learn to play an instrument or speak another language. Volunteer to help at your school or church or in your neighborhood. Sing in a choir. Try out for a team sport. You may find that you have talents you never knew about. You'll meet new people. And you'll feel good about yourself as you add to your knowledge and skills.

● Do what you say you're going to do. If your parents ask you to clean your room and you say you will, then do it. If you and a friend agree to meet at the mall at 4:00 P.M., be there at 4:00 P.M. The more you are a person of your word, the better you will feel about yourself.

There are many ways to improve your self-esteem. To learn more about it, check your local library for books on the subject. Talk to your parents, teachers, guidance counselors, or religious advisers about ways to build self-esteem. Since it's so important to your safety, developing your sense of self-esteem is worth the effort.

Preparation and Self-Esteem Can Help You Stay Safe
Lisa was selling candy outside the local supermarket to raise money for the school band. She had set up a small table and chair and had sold several boxes. But sales seemed to have slowed down in the past half hour, and there weren't many people around. Maybe it was time for Lisa to call her dad and ask him to come pick her up.

Suddenly Lisa looked up and saw a couple of boys approaching. She didn't know their names, but she recognized them as troublemakers in her neighborhood. She glanced inside the glass doors of the supermarket but couldn't see the security guard, who was usually standing just inside. She hoped the boys would just pass by and not pay any attention to her.

"What are you selling?" one of the boys asked as they got closer. His friend picked up a box of candy, turned it over a

couple of times, then casually dropped it back on the table.

"It's for the band," Lisa said in a small voice as she sank down into her chair. "Did you want to buy something?" That was a silly thing to say, she thought. Of course they didn't want to buy anything! She glanced toward the supermarket door again, hoping that the security guard would show up.

"Maybe." The boy looked around, as though checking to make sure no one else was near. "Maybe I'd rather have some of the money you've made so far. How about that?"

Lisa froze. She didn't know what to say. She glanced down at the shoe box she was using to keep the money in. Both boys followed her gaze.

"Like, maybe I'll take this box. Whadda ya say?" The boy reached over and picked up the shoe box. His friend grabbed a couple of boxes of candy and began backing away.

"Hey, thanks," the boy said. "You gonna be here tomorrow? Maybe we'll come back." His friend started laughing. Then they both took off running.

This was a scary situation for Lisa. However, there are some things she could have done differently, using the basics of self-defense:

● Lisa showed a good sense of awareness by setting up her table outside a supermarket, where she would probably be around a lot of other people. She could have talked to the security guard, though, and asked him to come out every now and then to check on her. Just because she was aware of him inside the store doesn't mean that he was aware of her outside.

● Lisa could have asked a friend to help her or joined up with another member of the band to sell the candy. Two or more people sitting at the table might not have looked like such an easy target to the boys.

● Once Lisa saw the boys approaching, she could have denied them a target by going inside the store. She might have also grabbed the shoe box with the money and taken it with her.

● When she was talking to the boys, Lisa could have stood up from her chair and looked them in the eye. She could have spoken in a loud voice. By shrinking into her chair and speaking softly, she appeared intimidated. She looked like an easy target.

Lisa did do the right thing, however, by not resisting when the boys took her money and some of the candy. Lisa's safety is more important than either the candy or the money. Remember, if you choose to fight someone, you risk getting hurt. Candy and money can be replaced. You can't.

ANSWERS TO "WHAT IF...?"

What if . . . you're walking home from school and you see an older boy coming toward you on the sidewalk. He's still a good distance away, but he has both hands in his pockets, and he's staring at you. You get a funny feeling in your stomach. It's daylight, there are cars passing by, and there are a couple of adults talking across the street. What do you do?

You can turn around and go back the way you came. Remember to use your peripheral vision to keep an eye on him. If there is a store nearby with people in it, you can go inside it until the boy passes by or you can cross the street (watch out for the cars!) to be closer to the adults or even go up to them and tell them you're nervous about the older boy.

Since it's daylight and there are lots of people around, you may think you have nothing to worry about and are just being paranoid. You may worry about looking silly if you cross the street or duck into a nearby store. But you've got that bad feeling in the pit of your stomach, and 99 percent of the time it's right. Better to worry about looking a little silly than to risk getting hurt. And better to use your body language and actions to send a strong message: "I see you sizing me up, and I'm the wrong person to choose as a victim."

What if you decide to avoid going near the boy and then nothing happens? Does that mean that you were safe all along and didn't need to take any action? Not necessarily. Maybe the boy was planning to make you a victim, but you denied him a target. Most of the time you will never know for sure if your awareness or self-esteem or any of the other skills you'll learn in this book have kept you from being a victim. Practice them anyway! They are the best way to ensure your safety.

What if . . . you're really late for soccer practice. It's faster to cut through the alleyway behind your building than to go around the block. But sometimes there are high school kids hanging around there, drinking and smoking. What do you do?

Better to be late for practice than to risk your safety. Once you get in the alley, you could find yourself alone and in trouble. Alleys are often full of cars and trash Dumpsters, which are ideal hiding places for dangerous people. Sure, you may have taken this short-cut before and been fine. But it takes only one time for things to go wrong and for you to get hurt. Stay away from places that you think may not be safe.

What if . . . you and a friend are waiting for your mom to pick you up just outside the movie theater. You notice a man standing nearby who's wearing a long overcoat even though it's not that cold and it's not raining. You have the feeling he's watching you, but he glances away whenever you look in his direction. What do you do?

Trust your instincts. If the man is making you uncomfortable, you can go back inside the movie theater lobby to wait for your ride. Or you can ask a theater employee to come outside with you while you wait. You may want to come up with an alternate waiting place, a nearby "safe haven" that you can go to in case you feel unsafe where you are. Discuss ahead of time where your parents should look for you if you have to leave the designated spot for some reason.

SETTING BOUNDARIES

2

WHAT IF...?

What if . . . you have a friend who keeps asking for your help with his computer programs. He has the manuals for the programs, but instead of using them, he's constantly calling you to talk him through them or to solve the problems he's having. He's your friend, but he's taking up a lot of your time with these calls. What do you do?

What if . . . you're waiting to cross a busy intersection and you see a homeless woman approaching you. She seems angry and is having an argument with an imaginary person. As she gets closer to you, she begins pointing at you and waving her arms in the air. What do you do?

WHAT IS A BOUNDARY?

A boundary marks the limit of something. For example, the boundary around a country marks the limit of that country's control. There is a boundary between the United States and Canada. When you cross that line, you travel from one country into another. Knowing where that boundary is and when you've crossed it is important because each country has different laws.

People have boundaries, too. There are physical boundaries, as in how close to you you'd like someone to be, and there are feelings boundaries, as in how you let other people treat you and whether they respect your feelings. You have the right to set boundaries and expect that others will abide by them.

You let people know where your boundaries are by using your voice and telling them. You cannot blame others for crossing the line when you have never told them where the line was. We often assume that other people already know what's okay with us and what's not. But we have to realize that we come from different backgrounds and different types of families. What is okay with you may not be okay with someone else.

Learning to set clear, strong boundaries with other people means learning how to tell them where your limits are, where you draw the line. We talk about the basics of boundary setting in this chapter and then use boundary setting in many different ways in each of the following chapters.

PHYSICAL BOUNDARIES

A physical boundary has to do with the distance between you and another person. An easy way to think of this distance is to imagine how many arm's lengths you are from someone.

> Stand next to a friend and hold out your arm so that you can just touch your friend's shoulder with your fingertips. Your friend is one arm's length away from you. Now, if your friend also holds out an arm and you both stand so that your fingertips are just touching, you are now two arm's lengths away from each other.

We each have a comfort zone, a certain amount of space around us that makes us feel comfortable. The size of this space can change, depending on where we are and who we are with. For example, you may feel fine squeezed up next to your best friend on a crowded bus, but sitting that close to a stranger or someone you think is weird may make you nervous.

That's Too Close

Ramal settled into his seat, placing his soda in the holder in the armrest and balancing the popcorn in his lap. Thomas sat beside him and handed Ramal some napkins. The movie theater was crowded, and they had found the last two seats together. Ramal was feeling pretty lucky until he noticed a man working his way past the other people in the row.

As the man squeezed past the boys, they looked at each other and made faces; the man smelled of cigarette smoke. He plopped down into the empty seat on the other side of Ramal.

Ramal suddenly felt as if he had been put into a cramped box. The theater seat, which had been so big and comfortable a moment before, now seemed very small. The man gave a long, nasty cough.

As the lights went down and the movie started, Ramal moved closer to Thomas; he wanted to put every possible inch between him and this stranger. He was probably going to get a crick in his neck from watching the movie at this angle, but he figured it was better than accidentally touching his smelly neighbor.

Thomas and the stranger were sitting equal distances from Ramal. However, Ramal had no problem sitting next to Thomas, because he knew and liked him. The comfort zone between Ramal and his friend was very small. But Ramal felt uneasy having the stranger so close to him. Ramal would have preferred a bigger comfort zone between himself and the stranger, and he tried to put more space between them by leaning as far away as possible.

It's important to know where your boundaries are and to be aware of people who cross them. Start noticing how much space you like to have between you and other people and how you feel when they get closer to you or move away from you.

Now imagine that outside your comfort zone is a larger space. This space is two arm's lengths away from your body. This is called your safe zone and is reserved for people you trust. Anyone within the safe zone is close enough to touch you, or grab you, or hit you. If someone is standing inside your safe zone and decides to

strike you, you're going to get hit. There's not enough distance for you to see it coming and get out of the way.

Of course there are times when you have to allow strangers into that zone—for example, when you're on a crowded bus or standing in line at the store or sitting in a movie theater. But these are places where you're not likely to be hurt or attacked, because there are a lot of other people around. Still, it's a good idea to be alert and keep an eye on strangers who are this close. Whenever possible, you will want to keep people you don't know or don't trust at least two arm's lengths away, well outside your safe zone.

Maintain Your Safe Zone

David stepped into the elevator and pushed a button. He'd spent the afternoon at the mall with his friends and was now hurrying to catch the bus home.

Two teenage boys were already in the elevator. They stared at David. One of them whispered something to the other and both laughed. David nervously moved to the opposite side of the elevator to put as much distance as possible between him and the other boys. He kept his eyes glued to the elevator control panel.

"Boo!" one of the boys shouted, and David nearly jumped out of his skin. The teenagers doubled over with laughter. David broke out in a sweat, and his mind began to race, trying to think of what he could do. He felt trapped. He looked up at the panel of buttons to see which one was lit—three more floors to go.

Suddenly the elevator stopped, and the boys moved toward the doors, blocking David's way. David felt his panic rising. The boys glared at him before finally leaving the elevator.

"Hey, we'll be watching you," one boy said threateningly as the doors started to close. David stood still, unable to move. When he finally reached the street, he looked around to see if the teenagers might be hiding, waiting to surprise him. Then he ran as fast as he could to the bus stop.

The comfort zone David would have liked between him and the other boys was much bigger than the inside of the elevator. Even though he moved as far away from them as he could, he still didn't feel comfortable. But he did maintain a safe zone, keeping himself out of arm's reach of the two boys. Confined spaces like elevators, alleys, and cars can be very dangerous, because it's hard to keep a safe zone between you and another person. You need to be especially aware in small spaces and plan for the possibility that you might need to get out of that space in a hurry.

Elevators can be scary when you're stuck with people who make you uneasy. It's always a good idea to look inside an elevator before getting on. If you don't feel comfortable with the people you see in there, don't get on. Listen to your gut, and wait for the next one. If you're already in an elevator and you feel uncomfortable with a passenger who just got on, get off as soon as possible (target denial). Push the button for the very next floor, and get right off.

When you're in an elevator, stand next to the button panel so you can push any button you need as well as block someone else from pushing the stop button. This also puts you closer to the door, so you can exit quickly. Keep an eye on the other passengers in the elevator and keep as much distance as you can between you and them.

In this instance David could have pushed a button for the next floor and gotten off the elevator there. This would have allowed him to catch a different elevator to get down to the street level. If he believed that the boys might try to follow him or ambush him, David could also have chosen to go back up to the mall, where there were other people. He could have waited awhile in the mall before heading home again, or he could have called home and asked someone to pick him up. He also could have talked to a mall security guard. Perhaps a guard could have escorted him down to the bus or even called a police car to give David a ride home.

If you feel uneasy, do not hesitate to seek help. Don't be afraid of looking silly. Your safety is too important. Do whatever you have to do to stay safe.

HOW TO SET A PHYSICAL BOUNDARY

Setting a physical boundary means keeping a safe distance between yourself and another person. For example, you can set a boundary by taking a step or two back or going a little out of your way in order to create more distance. It may mean leaving a place where you no longer feel safe.

You can also set a boundary by using your voice and body language. It is okay to tell people that they are too close and to ask them to stop or to step back. When you set a boundary, it is important that your voice, your body language, and your attitude all send the same message to the other person. For example, if you tell someone to leave you alone, but you're smiling or giggling or looking away from the person you're speaking to, that person is not going to take you seriously. You're giving the other person a mixed signal, because your words are saying one thing ("leave me alone") but your body language is saying something else ("I'm giggling, so I don't mean it," or "I'm looking away, so I must not be serious," or "I'm smiling, which means I'm not really angry").

If you want someone to know you're serious, you have to act serious—from the top of your head to the bottom of your toes. Your words and your body language have to give the same message.

When setting a boundary with someone, you need to do the following:

● Make sure you have the other person's attention. Look him or her in the eye.

● Be direct. Say what you mean as simply as you can.

● Be consistent. Make sure that your facial expression, tone of voice, and body language let the other person know that you're serious and mean what you're saying.

● Make a statement ("Stop"). Don't ask a question ("Stop, okay?").

● Don't apologize. You have a right to set a boundary when you feel uncomfortable and you don't have to be sorry for it.

Say "Stop" to Set a Boundary

Kyle was on vacation with his family. They were wandering around a shopping center, looking for gifts to bring home.

"Hey, kid, have you seen one of these?" A thin man was suddenly standing in front of Kyle. He was holding some sort of computer game in his hands and was trying to show Kyle how it worked.

Kyle glanced at the toy. It looked old and cheap. "Umm, no, I'm not interested," Kyle mumbled. He started to walk by, but the man stepped in front of him again, blocking his way.

"I've only got a couple of these left. I'll sell you this one for almost nothing."

"I don't want it," Kyle said. He glanced around for his parents but couldn't see them in the crowd. He was starting to get nervous.

The man was hovering over Kyle, talking nonstop. "I'll throw in an extra set of batteries. You can play it on the plane ride home. I'll even give you a second one for half price."

It didn't seem that the man could get any closer to Kyle, but he did. His nose was practically touching Kyle's nose.

Kyle took a big step back and said in a loud voice, "Stop." The man paused for a moment and finally looked up from the game. Kyle looked him in the eye. "I said no."

"Hey, kid, I'm just trying to make a living here. You'd really be helping me out if you could buy one or two—"

"No!" Kyle shouted. "I don't want to buy anything. Leave me alone!"

"Okay, okay. Never mind. There's no reason to get so upset," the man said as he started backing away.

Kyle tried to be polite and nicely told the man that he wasn't interested. When the man didn't listen, Kyle had to set a stronger boundary. Even though they were in a crowded area, the man was a stranger to Kyle, and he was too close. Kyle's parents weren't nearby, so Kyle had to take care of himself. Notice all the things he did:

● He stepped back to create more distance between himself and the man. Kyle needed to get the man outside his safe zone and make sure he was out of arm's reach. He stepped back until the man was at a safer distance.

● Kyle used his voice and spoke loudly. When that didn't work, he raised his voice even more and shouted.

● He made certain that he looked the man in the eye, so the man could tell that Kyle was serious.

● Kyle made a statement instead of asking a question. He said,

"Leave me alone," instead of "Will you leave me alone?" Kyle had already told the man he wasn't interested in the game. But the man wasn't listening. If someone doesn't listen to you, it's time to stop being nice; it's time to be direct. Tell that person what you want him or her to do ("Stop"; "Step back"; "Leave me alone"; "Go away"; "Stay away from me"; "Don't touch me"). Use whichever phrase sounds best to you.

● Kyle did not apologize. He has the right to shop without being bothered. He has the right to tell the man to go away. He tried twice to tell the man politely he wasn't interested, but when that didn't work, Kyle had to be direct. There was no reason for him to be sorry.

It can be hard to set a physical boundary with someone. It can be hard to tell another person to back up or to stay away from you. But you have a right to be safe in this world. And you have a right to protect yourself by keeping a safe distance between you and those who might threaten you.

The important thing with boundaries is to know where your limits are and then to make them clear to other people. You cannot expect others to respect your boundaries if you've never clearly expressed them. Also, knowing your own boundaries helps you recognize when they are being crossed or ignored.

Be aware of someone who crosses or ignores a boundary that you've set, either a feelings boundary or a physical boundary. This can be a warning of potential trouble, because that person is not listening to you and is not respecting your rights.

Have a friend walk toward you from across the room. Practice saying "Stop" when she gets to a distance of two arm's lengths. If you giggle when you do this, it won't work as well. So practice good body language and a serious facial expression. When you're comfortable saying "Stop" to your friend, try saying "Stop" and then say, "Take a step back." Try practicing this exercise until it's easy to do.

Next have your friend walk quickly toward you and practice saying "Stop" very loudly. Do you notice that when someone is moving quickly, you have to speak even sooner to get that person to stop before he or she gets too close?

Finally, practice saying "Stop" and "Don't come any closer" using a different tone of voice. This time keep your voice quiet but also low and very serious.

It's important to keep your body steady as you do this exercise. If your body feels that way, it will help you speak with confidence. Pay attention during this exercise to such common mistakes as rocking on your feet, speaking very quickly, not making eye contact, and laughing.

FEELINGS BOUNDARIES

A feelings boundary is where you draw the line in terms of how you let other people treat you. Setting a feelings boundary is a way to let people know how you want your thoughts and feelings respected.

For instance, let's say that your sister likes to borrow your clothes. Perhaps you've told her that it's fine for her to borrow them *as long as she asks you.* That's a boundary that you've set up. When she takes your clothes without asking, she's overstepped that boundary, and that makes you uncomfortable. When someone reads your diary, or calls you stupid, or continues to behave a certain way when you've asked him or her to stop, that person is not respecting your feelings and is crossing your feelings boundaries.

As with physical boundaries, feelings boundaries can change depending on who you're with and what the circumstances are. You may choose to share what's in your diary with your best friend but be horrified if your brother or sister reads it without your per-mission. You might be happy to loan a favorite book or CD to your next-door neighbor but would turn down the same request from a kid at school that you barely know.

Sometimes it's easier to set boundaries with people we don't know than with family or close friends. With strangers we're not as concerned about hurting their feelings or having to deal with them later. But no matter whom you're dealing with—family, friend, or stranger—it is important to get your message across clearly.

If you need to set a feelings boundary with someone, start off by explaining how you feel:

"I feel uncomfortable . . ."

Now tell that person what caused you to feel this way:

". . . when you talk about me in front of other people as though I'm not there."

Then offer a solution:

"Would you please talk to me and not ignore me?"

We call this the Magic Formula. Here are a few more examples to give you a better idea of how this works:

"I feel angry when you borrow my clothes without asking. Would you please ask first? If I'm not around to ask, please don't borrow anything."

"I feel hurt when I tell you a secret and you tell other people. Would you please not tell my secrets, or ask me first if it's okay to tell things I've told you?"

"I feel bad when you interrupt me all the time. I'll listen to you, but would you please let me finish talking first?"

If you speak to people in an accusing way—

"You never listen . . ."

"You're always nagging . . ."

"You make me so mad . . ."

—they will tune you out. They may react angrily—

"You think you're always right, don't you?"

"Well, that's because you're so lazy . . ."

"If you would just try harder . . ."

Pretty soon no one is listening, everyone is angry, and nothing gets done.

Boundary setting is not always easy, but the more you do it, the better you will become at it. Start by simply noticing where your boundaries are. You don't have to do anything about them at first—just know where they are. When other people cross your boundaries, try to figure out why they did it. Was it because you didn't make it clear to them where you draw the line? Or have you set boundaries that they are simply ignoring?

Boundaries Come in All Flavors

Allison looked over the list of flavors at the yogurt shop. Candace stood next to her, also looking over the selection. Candace's family had just moved into the neighborhood, and she was new at school, but the two girls were quickly becoming friends.

"Know what you want?" Allison asked.

"Yeah. I'm going for the strawberry with crumbled Oreos on top," Candace said. "Let me guess. You're getting vanilla with chocolate sauce."

"Absolutely." Allison stepped up to the counter and placed her order. Candace gave hers, too, and they started collecting napkins and spoons. Allison pulled out some money from her pocket and paid for her yogurt. She was counting her change when Candace turned to her.

"Darn. Allison, can I borrow a dollar? I thought I had enough, but the Oreos cost extra."

Allison paused. She didn't like loaning out money. In fact, her parents had taught her it was rude to ask other people for money. She thought about saying she didn't have a dollar, but Candace had clearly seen a couple of bills in Allison's hand.

"Umm, let me see . . . Yeah, I've got a dollar." Allison reluctantly handed a dollar to Candace.

"Thanks. I guess this is what friends are for. I'll pay you back

later." Candace smiled, then paid for her scoop of yogurt.

Allison and Candace have different feelings about borrowing and loaning money. Neither is right or wrong; they're just different. However, if Allison doesn't speak up about how she feels, Candace will never know, and she'll continue asking to borrow money. The stronger Allison's self-esteem is, the easier it will be for her to tell Candace how she feels. Allison has the right to ask for what she wants.

Allison could use the Magic Formula with Candace. For example, she could say to Candace: "I like you, and I like having you as a friend, but I feel uncomfortable when you ask to borrow money from me. Would you please bring enough money with you when we go somewhere together?" Allison might be willing to loan Candace money in an emergency, and she might even tell her that. But until Allison sets a boundary, she can't get mad at Candace for not knowing that it bothers Allison.

It is a fact of life, however, that there are some people who will not respect your boundaries, no matter how clear you are in setting them and no matter how many times you try to do so. It's up to you to decide whether or not you want these people in your life.

WHAT IF YOU SET A BOUNDARY AND PEOPLE STILL DON'T DO WHAT YOU ASK?

If your boundaries are being ignored by a family member or someone else you see over and over again, you can decide to change the way you respond to that behavior. You may try to spend less time with that person. You may also want to get help from others who are having a similar problem with this person and see if you can come up with ways to deal with it.

Let's say your older sister is always late picking you up—at school or at the mall or from band practice. You've asked her to be on time, your parents have told her to be more punctual, but nothing works. Here are some things you might do:

● Try to arrange rides with other people.

● Ask her to come earlier than you need her to. For instance, ask her to pick you up at six-fifteen, even though she doesn't have to be there until six-thirty.

● Tell your parents how you feel, and ask them to help you come up with other solutions. Don't rely on your sister if being on time is really important to you or if waiting for her makes you feel unsafe.

Boundary setting is something you'll need to practice all your life—with parents, relatives, friends, teachers, coaches, coworkers, and, someday, your own children. It's a skill that comes in handy in everyday life, not just in self-defense. It's never too early to start learning how to do it.

ANSWERS TO "WHAT IF...?"

What if . . . you have a friend who keeps asking for your help with his computer programs. He has the manuals for the programs, but instead of using them, he's constantly calling you to talk him through them or to solve the problems he's having. He's your friend, but he's taking up a lot of your time with these calls. What do you do?

You need to use your voice to set a boundary with your friend. He doesn't know he's being a pest if you don't tell him. You could also avoid him and his calls, but that's a short-term solution, since you probably won't be able to avoid him forever. You might suggest that he take a class to learn how to use his programs. Or you can continue to help him but charge him for your time. Perhaps he could pay you by the hour; there are people who make very good livings helping others learn to use their computers. This could be the beginning of your career!

What if . . . you're waiting to cross a busy intersection and you see a homeless woman approaching you. She seems angry and is having an argument with an imaginary person. As she gets closer to you, she begins pointing at you and waving her arms in the air. What do you do?

First, be sure you keep at least two arm's lengths (the safe zone) from the woman. You don't want her to get close enough to reach you. If there is any type of safe place nearby—a store, a school, a police car, a crossing guard—head for that. But don't turn your back completely on the woman. Use your peripheral vision to check on whether she follows you or to see if she's coming any closer. Make sure that you don't get trapped between her and the busy intersection; you'll want a way out that doesn't involve running into traffic.

It's probably not a good idea to try talking to her. She doesn't appear to be making sense, and she may not even hear you. Some homeless people have mental illnesses, which can make them unpredictable. It's safer to keep away from people who are acting strangely. If you think someone needs help, tell a police officer or a social worker or call 911. But in face-to-face situations with the homeless, it is better to stay out of reach.

If the woman continues coming toward you, you may need to run away. If you have to run, you will have a head start if you've made certain to keep at least two arm's lengths away from the woman. If there are other people around, you may want to call out to them for help. As soon as you notice the woman, start thinking about your options. This will help if you have to decide quickly what action to take.

My Body Is Mine

3

WHAT IF...?

What if . . . your sister has a habit of pinching you hard whenever she thinks she's losing an argument?

What if . . . you're riding in a car with your uncle, and he pats your leg, then reaches up and squeezes the inside of your thigh?

What if . . . you're waiting to use the diving board at the local pool and an older kid in line after you slaps you on the behind?

WHAT IS UNWANTED TOUCH?

Being touched is often a pleasant experience. Babies need to be held and hugged, just as much as they need sleep and food.

Putting your arm around your best friend or kissing your parents good-night are ways that you show affection to those you care about. When you're tired or hurt or scared or sad, it can be nice to cry on someone's shoulder and get a reassuring pat on the back.

But sometimes you just don't want to be touched. Maybe you're in a bad mood and you don't feel like having anyone around. Or perhaps there is a particular person who gives you the creeps and you don't like being touched by him or her at all. This is called unwanted touch. It can include hugging, pinching, playing with your hair, tickling, or kissing. You have the right to set boundaries when it comes to people touching your body. You have the right to tell someone "No" or "Stop" if you don't want that person to touch you.

Just as you do with feelings boundaries, you need to let other people know what kind of touching is okay with you and what kind of touching you don't like.

STOPPING UNWANTED TOUCH

In order to stop another person from touching you in a way that you don't like, you will need to set a firm boundary (see Chapter Two for more tips on setting boundaries). The following are some good ideas for stopping unwanted touch:

● Tell the person "Stop." Look him or her in the eye. Don't laugh or smile as you say this. Be consistent. Act serious so the person knows you are serious.

● If the person continues touching you, take his or her hands or arms off your body and again say "Stop."

● If the person continues, move out of reach; stand up and step away. Look the person in the eye and say that you don't like what he or she is doing and you want it to stop. Get away from the situation as soon as possible and tell a trusted adult.

● If the person gets angry and threatens you or someone you care about, tell a trusted adult what happened.

A trusted adult is someone whom you can talk to and who cares about you and your safety. This should be someone you are comfortable sharing your feelings with. It is important for you to have one or more trusted adults in your life. This could be a parent, a grandparent, an aunt or uncle, an adult brother or sister, a neighbor, a teacher, or a religious leader (like a priest or nun, minister, or rabbi).

There are times when it's necessary to seek the help of a trusted adult. Some situations cannot be solved by you alone. You may want to read Chapter Seven—"Getting Help"—for some guidelines on when to seek help and how to go about asking for it.

Some forms of unwanted touch can be avoided with creative movements like this one:

Stand face-to-face with a friend. Have your friend raise her arms and come toward you as though she were going to give you a big hug. But before your friend can get her arms around you, grab both her hands and hold them in front of you. She can't hug you now, because you're holding her hands.

Maybe there is someone you know who's always smothering you in big bear hugs, but you don't really like it. Perhaps he or she is a friend or a relative whom you care about, and you don't want to hurt his or her feelings. You can use a very gentle version of this maneuver to avoid the hug but still give the other person some contact with you.

You can also try this: Stand next to your friend, shoulder to shoulder. Have your friend put one arm around you and give you a sideways hug. You can get out of this hug by grabbing your friend's hand and lifting her arm over your head. You can give her arm back to her and step away, or you can continue to stand next to her and hold her hand so that she can't put her arm around you again.

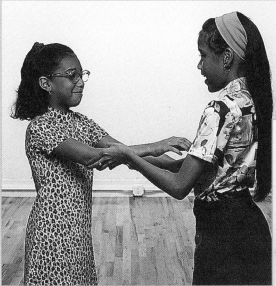

Unwanted Touch from Other Kids

Kids can be very cruel to one another. Much of this cruelty comes in the form of name calling and other hurtful words, but sometimes it is physical. Pinching, pulling hair, grabbing another person's buttocks, snapping bra straps—all these are examples of unwanted touch you might experience from another child.

If this has ever happened to you, you may have been afraid to say anything. You may have been embarrassed or not wanted the other person to see how much he or she was bothering you. But not doing or saying anything often encourages the behavior. If the person bothering you thinks that nothing will happen to him or her, there is no reason to stop tormenting you. It gives that person a feeling of power and control when you don't say anything.

No one has the right to touch you against your will. You can use your voice to set a boundary and to draw attention to the behavior. You may also need to use your voice to tell others in authority, like teachers, bus drivers, and coaches. They can take disciplinary action, such as notifying the child's parents of his or her conduct, and can make sure it doesn't keep happening.

Stop . . . and I Mean It

Josh was watching television one day when his older brother, Aaron, and Aaron's friend Damon came into the room. They were laughing loudly, and Josh turned the volume up slightly so he could hear the TV.

"Hey, little brother. Whatcha watching?" Aaron came into the den and plopped down in a nearby chair.

"Yeah, squirt, anything good on?" Damon sat next to Josh on the couch.

"I don't know. I can't hear anything with you talking," Josh said.

"Hey, Damon, you want one of those burritos we've got in the freezer?" Aaron asked.

"Sure, nuke me two of 'em," Damon said.

Josh wished they would keep quiet so he could watch his show.

Aaron headed back to the kitchen. Damon moved closer to Josh. Josh ignored him, hoping Damon would leave him alone. But then Damon put his arm around Josh and started rubbing his knuckles hard on the top of Josh's head.

"Hey, quit it, okay?" Josh laughed a little and tried to squirm out of Damon's grip. Josh didn't want to let on how much he hated this, because he was afraid that would give Damon the upper hand.

"What's the matter, squirt? Can't take it, huh?" Damon started tickling him, too.

"Damon, come on, cut it out." Josh was really ticklish, and he couldn't help giggling, even though he was feeling more and more angry. *"I'm trying to watch TV."*

"Okay, pipsqueak. Watch your show. I gotta get something to eat." Damon let him go and got up to join Aaron in the kitchen. Josh pulled his shirt down and tried to fix his hair, which Damon had messed up. He felt so angry. One of these days, Josh thought, I'm not going to take this anymore.

"One of these days . . . ," Josh thinks. Well, thinking isn't going to change Damon's behavior. Josh needs to let Damon know that he doesn't like being touched in such a rough way.

Josh needs to tell Damon to stop. And he needs to do it without smiling or laughing. He also needs to do it when Damon isn't tickling him, so he won't giggle either.

Since Damon is older and probably bigger than Josh, Josh may want to be out of Damon's reach when he talks to him about this. Josh will need to make sure he has Damon's attention and to look Damon in the eye when he tells him that he doesn't like the knuckles and the tickling.

When he talks to Damon, Josh may want someone else present—perhaps his brother, Aaron, or one of his parents. That way Damon can't claim that Josh never told him to stop.

If Damon continues with the unwanted touch, Josh may have to ask for his parents' help in stopping it. Perhaps Damon won't be welcome at their house until he agrees to leave Josh alone. Josh has the right to feel safe in his own home.

A lot of these suggestions will also work when dealing with unwanted touch from a teammate or from another child at school or on a bus. You will be amazed how people respond when you look them in the eye and tell them "Stop." Especially if you are consistent—when your face, your voice, and your body language tell another person that you mean business.

Unwanted Touch from Adults

There are adults in your life who have some authority over you—

parents, relatives, siblings, your teacher or coach, your doctor, baby-sitters, tutors, religious leaders (priests, ministers, rabbis). For the most part these are people who are concerned with your well-being. Their job is to help you in some way and to protect you.

Since these are all family members and friends, it can sometimes be difficult to talk honestly with them, because you don't want to hurt their feelings or make them angry. However, there are certain boundaries that even these adults cannot cross. One of those boundaries is touching you in a way that you don't like.

Remember, unwanted touch can be anything from tickling or pinching to hugging or kissing. If certain touching is not okay with you, then you need to tell the other people. If they truly love you and care about you, they will stop doing something that makes you uncomfortable.

There are also some adults who want to hurt children and seek out those they think won't tell. These people may take a long time in getting to know you, slowly going from friendly hugging to more intimate touching. They will try to convince you to keep the touching a secret, because they are afraid of being found out. They may even threaten you with harm or threaten to harm those you love.

When someone's physical affection is making you uncomfortable, you must get help as soon as possible. Tell someone! Do not be a silent victim. If you don't tell, the touching probably will not stop. (See Chapter Seven—"Getting Help.")

Saying "No" to Unwanted Touch
Debby stretched with all her might to touch the edge of the

pool. As she came up out of the water, her teammates were screaming and cheering above her. They helped her out of the swimming pool, and then Debby was engulfed in wet hugs. This was the first of many wins, they all hoped.

Debby tensed slightly as Coach Moore came up to congratulate her. As usual, one hand rested on her behind while he hugged her. Debby tried to move away, but he put one arm around her waist and kept her next to him.

"That was great! Everyone, you all did a great job! Congratulations." Coach Moore was laughing and high-fiving his swimmers. He bent over to Debby and gave her a quick kiss on the cheek. "You were terrific," he said.

Debby thanked him, then pulled away. She picked up a towel and joined the rush of other girls on their way to the showers. Despite the big win, she felt sad and scared. Tears were welling in her eyes.

She enjoyed being on the swim team, but she was starting to feel sick to her stomach every time she came to practice. Debby cringed whenever Coach Moore came near her. She was tired of feeling so icky. Maybe she should just quit the team.

Debby could choose to quit the team. Of course, that would mean giving up something she really enjoys. Another option would be to talk to other girls on the team and see if any of them had also experienced unwanted touching from the coach. If so, they could decide to confront Coach Moore together. They could set a boundary and explain to him how uncomfortable his actions made them feel and let him know he needed to change his behavior.

Debby could also tell a trusted adult—a parent, teacher, youth counselor, or relative. Perhaps that adult could help Debby weigh her options and decide what action she wants to take. If she chooses to speak with Coach Moore about the problem, this adult could go with her. Having a friend present could give Debby the courage and support she needs to confront the coach. This would also let Coach Moore know that his behavior is not a secret and other people are aware of his conduct.

It could be that Coach Moore is unaware of how his touching makes Debby feel. Once she tells him, he may agree to change his behavior. Then Debby could stay on the team and see if he does indeed behave differently.

Or Coach Moore could deny Debby's feelings. He might tell her that she's overreacting and that he was just being affectionate with her. He might tell her that she's being silly. But Debby has a right to her feelings, and she also has a right to tell him to stop touching her in a way that makes her uncomfortable.

In any case, if his behavior does not change, Debby can choose to quit the team or to tell others in authority. This decision definitely needs to be made with a trusted adult. If Debby hasn't confided in a trusted adult before this point, now would be the time to do it.

There are times when it is necessary for adults to touch you in private places. For example, when you go to the doctor, he or she may need to lift up your shirt to hear your breathing through the stethoscope. But that kind of touch is never a secret, and if you ever feel uncomfortable about the way a doctor is touching you, you can tell him or her to stop. And, if there isn't a nurse already in the room with you, you can ask for one if you feel uncomfortable.

A good rule to keep in mind: Any part of your body that a bathing suit covers is private. You have the right to decide who touches you there.

UNWANTED TOUCH FROM STRANGERS

A stranger should never be allowed to touch you in a way that you don't like. With a stranger, you will need to use all the self-defense skills we've mentioned so far:

● Keep at least two arm's lengths away, so the stranger cannot enter your safe zone.

● Use your voice to set a strong, clear boundary by telling the stranger to stay away from you or to leave you alone.

● Use your voice to tell a trusted adult about the stranger. You may want to read Chapter Eight for more tips on dealing with strangers.

Practice these exercises with a friend or a trusted adult:

Have your friend place a hand on your knee. Take his hand, lift it off your knee, and place it on his own leg. Say

"Stop" as you do this and make sure that your face and your voice are serious. Look your friend in the eye so he knows you mean it. Even though this is just practice, don't giggle or smile. Ask your friend how it felt to be on the receiving end of your boundary setting. Try practicing this exercise three or four times; it should get easier each time you do it. Then change roles and let your friend practice, too.

This kind of boundary setting exercise can be difficult to do. Many children grow up with rules about being polite to adults. You may have been taught not to say something if it will hurt someone else's feelings. You may even think it is rude to tell someone to stop and to remove his or her hand from your body. Most of the time we should practice being polite. But your safety always comes first. You always have permission to put your safety above someone else's feelings. As you start setting these boundaries, it gets easier and easier.

Have your friend continue to try to grab your knee. Practice moving out of reach and making it clear that you want him to stop touching you. Again, change roles and have your friend practice.

Practice this skill whenever someone touches you in a way you don't like. It's okay if it does not feel great. Over time and with practice, boundary setting will feel more comfortable and will even increase your self-esteem.

Each time you have to set a boundary and you feel uncomfortable or need a boost of courage, remember this: When you set a boundary, you treat yourself with respect, and that means you know how valuable and special you really are.

Answers to "What if...?"

What if . . . your sister has a habit of pinching you hard whenever she thinks she's losing an argument?

You may want to move out of your sister's reach and then tell her she needs to stop pinching you. Let her know that you are serious and that you won't put up with it anymore. You might give her one more chance before you call in a higher authority (meaning a parent or some other adult). Siblings may be especially difficult to deal with. But you need to set boundaries with them, just as you would with other kids or with adults, and make it clear what you will and will not put up with.

What if . . . you're riding in a car with your uncle, and he pats your leg, then reaches up and squeezes the inside of your thigh?

Grab your uncle's hand, and take it off your thigh. At the same time, tell him that you don't like him touching you there. Be serious when you tell him this: no laughing or giggling. If he tries to laugh it off, tell him again in a very serious voice that you do not want him touching you.

You might also let him know that you will tell someone else, such as a parent, if he doesn't stop. Sometimes threatening to tell will get the person to stop right away, because he or she doesn't want anyone else to know.

If someone asks you to keep it a secret or tries to scare you so that you won't tell, you could also lie and say you won't tell if that person stops. Remember, you can say or do whatever you need to make the person stop. Then leave. You need to tell a trusted adult what has happened as soon as you can.

If anyone continues to try to touch you in ways that you don't like or if he or she asks you to keep this a secret between the two of you, you need to tell a trusted adult immediately.

What if . . . you're waiting to use the diving board at the local pool and an older kid in line after you slaps you on the behind?

You can ignore it if you want. But this may encourage that person to continue picking on you. You can also face the older kid and use your voice to tell him or her to stop and to leave you alone.

If there are other people around, especially lifeguards, you may want to speak loudly so that they are aware of the older kid's behavior. If the child touches you again, after you've told him or her to stop, it may be time to tell the lifeguard or another adult.

If you do not want to confront the older kid, you can try some target denial: Let the kid go ahead of you in line, so that he or she is no longer behind you, or give up your place in line and go to the back. This may solve your immediate problem, but chances are you'll have to face this kid again at some point.

BULLIES

4

WHAT IF...?

What if . . . you ride the bus to school and there's a kid or group of kids who are always picking on you, calling you names, and stealing your things?

What if . . . someone in your class insists that you let him or her cheat off your test and, if you don't let him or her cheat, he or she threatens not to be your friend anymore and to tell everyone your big secret?

What if . . . a bully corners you in the locker room, picks up a baseball bat, and begins to taunt you by swinging at your knees and barely missing them?

WHY ARE SOME PEOPLE BULLIES?

First of all, let's set the record straight. Bullies are cowards. They make other people their victims because they fear being victims themselves. Sometimes bullies are also being victimized by others. They bully someone weaker than they are so they can feel better about themselves. They select those they think are weaker so they can guarantee they'll come out the winners. It is also not uncommon for a group of bullies to gang up on one person, to make it more likely they will win.

Some bullies are big and use the threat of physical harm to make people do what they want. They learn early on that their size or strength can be used to their advantage. Despite the tough language, you will find that this type of bully always picks on people physically smaller or weaker—never on someone he or she believes could be a real threat to him or her. If such a bully doesn't think he'll win in a fair fight, he will resort to dirty tactics. For instance, he may sneak up from behind and ambush you or gang up with a buddy so the odds are in his favor.

There are others, though, who use verbal threats to bully their victims. They may harass you with teasing and name calling. Or they may threaten you not with physical harm but with telling your secrets or by spreading lies about you or by withholding their friendship. This is called blackmail. Such a bully will use your fears and weaknesses against you. This is the type of person who says things like "If you were really my friend, you would . . ." or "If you don't do this, then I'll tell everyone . . ."

Bullies are not courageous. The dictionary defines *courage* as "bravery," as being brave enough to do what one feels to be right. But bullies are not interested in doing the right thing. They are interested only in winning. Bullies never develop courage.

It does take courage, though, to stand up to a bully. And bullies don't exist only in schoolyards. You will encounter them in many different forms throughout your life. So it's important that you learn to deal with them now, because they aren't going away.

How to Avoid a Bully

● The first step in avoiding a bully is target denial. Don't give the bully a victim. Be the kind of person that bullies would rather avoid.

● Work on building your self-esteem. The more confident you are, the less attractive you will be to a bully.

● Use your voice. Bullies tend to avoid people who speak up and stand their ground. Don't be intimidated into silence.

● Build a strong support system of family and friends. It's much easier for a bully to go after someone who is isolated and alone than someone who has friends who will stick by him or her.

● Be willing to stand up for others who are victimized by bullies. It will send a message that you do not put up with bullying, even when you're not the one being bullied. And those you help may come to your aid someday.

How to Deal with a Bully

Sometimes, though, despite your best efforts, you may still end up a target. While you cannot control the actions of bullies, you do have control over how you respond to them. Giving in to their demands only teaches them that you are an easy target and encourages them to keep coming back. Standing up to bullies, which is understandably frightening, is the best way to stop them. And the sooner you set a boundary—make it clear that you will not put up with their bullying—the sooner it will stop. Sadly, the bully will probably move on to bother someone else, but at least you will be left alone.

● Realize that the bully is trying to get a response from you—anger, tears, embarrassment. The less bothered you seem, the more frustrating it is for the bully.

● Remember that words are just words. Teasing and name calling can't hurt you unless you let them. This is where self-esteem helps, because if you can remember all the good things about yourself, it's easier to ignore what a bully says.

● Use your voice. Try humor or agreeing with a bully to talk your way out of a situation. This is called de-escalating, which means "calming things down."

● Find strength and support in numbers. Ask your friends to help by walking home with you or sticking by you at recess or at the bus stop—any of the places where the bully likes to harass you. Bullies don't like being outnumbered.

● Listen to your gut. If a bully is trying to talk you into doing something you don't want to do or something you know is wrong, stand your ground. Don't give in to what the bully wants.

● Try every option you and trusted adults can think of besides fighting. Remember, if you fight, you risk getting hurt. Don't resort to fighting unless nothing else works and you are in physical danger. See Chapter Nine on tips for defending yourself if attacked.

De-escalate Confrontations with Bullies
The bus pulled up to the stop and Bobby paused for a moment before stepping aboard, preparing himself for what he knew was coming. As soon as he climbed in, the torment began.

"Whoa, everybody to this side of the bus or Lardo's gonna tip us over!" one boy yelled.

"Hey, Moby Dick, how many boxes of cereal did you have for breakfast today?" another one chimed in.

"Only three. I'm on a diet," Bobby answered. He smiled, even though the teasing hurt. He good-naturedly punched the nearest boy in the arm. "Hey, did you guys see the game last night on ESPN?"

Mentioning the baseball game got them talking about sports and took the focus off Bobby. His father had suggested this strategy for dealing with the cruel jokes: Keep a sense of humor, and try to change the subject. It worked most of the time, but it was really hard.

Bobby listened to the talk of balls and strikes and home runs, but deep inside he was still hurt by the teasing. Quietly he went over his mental list of things he liked about himself. Some people were never going to see him as anything but fat. But that didn't mean that Bobby had to think of himself that way, that he wasn't as good as other people because he was overweight. He decided to add "a great sense of humor" to his list of good qualities and took his seat on the bus.

There are some people who just seem to attract the attention of bullies more often than others. They include kids who are overweight or shy, or those with physical challenges, or kids with ethnic, racial, or religious backgrounds different from most of the other people in their community. Bullies seem to especially enjoy picking on things about you that you can't change. This is where your self-esteem becomes important.

For instance, Bobby has learned the hard way that his weight makes him a target for teasing and bullying. But he's also learned some tricks for dealing with it. He knows that there is more to him than his weight.

Bobby didn't give the other kids the response they were looking for—he didn't get upset or angry. He went along with the joking, not letting their words hurt him. They lost interest in teasing Bobby and were open to changing the subject when he started talking about sports. This strategy is called de-escalation or redirection. Instead of confronting the person and saying, "Stop calling me fat," you can de-escalate by agreeing—"Yeah, I am fat"—and then redirecting the conversation to another topic, such as sports.

Examples of de-escalation are:

● "You are tougher than I am, so we don't need to fight."

● "You're right, I am ugly. Why don't I leave so you don't have to look at me?"

Examples of redirecting are:

● Talking about sports

● Asking questions about movies or music ("Have you heard [the latest CD]?")

● Finding something in common you both dislike, such as homework or a band

It can be tempting to join in when others are teasing someone.

Many people would rather join in than risk being teased themselves. Don't do it! You should know that people behave differently in groups than when they are alone. It is very hard to stand up to a group, particularly when fitting into the group is important to you. However, good self-esteem will help you resist behaving in a way that you know is wrong.

Does this mean you should intervene to stop other bullies? Couldn't that get you into a fight rather than avoid one? Coming to another person's aid is a difficult decision, and yes, it might get you into a confrontation with someone. If you have warning that something is up, speak to your parents or a trusted adult and make a plan.

You need to make sure that by helping someone else, you won't get hurt, too. Sometimes helping means contacting someone who is older and better able to help than you are. Sometimes it means being a good witness and remembering carefully everything that happens.

Saying "No" to Bullies Who Use Blackmail
Liz's mom had sent her to the neighborhood grocery store to buy a few items for dinner that night. She'd also given Liz some extra money to buy a snack. Liz was trying to decide what she wanted when someone suddenly put her hands over her eyes and said, "Guess who?" Liz was so surprised she nearly screamed, but then she recognized her friend Heidi's giggles and turned around.

Heidi was always sneaking up on people. She loved playing

practical jokes. Some people thought she was a pain in the neck, but Liz thought she was exciting.

"I can't decide which candy bar to get." Liz showed Heidi her two choices.

"Wow, tough decision." Heidi shook her head in mock seriousness. "Why don't you just get them both?"

"Can't afford it."

"So, why don't you just drop one in your pocket, pay for the other one, and you're outta here?" Heidi made it sound so simple!

"Yeah, right. I'm gonna shoplift a candy bar." Liz started to put one of the candy bars back on the shelf.

"No, I'm serious. The chocolate bar is small. You just put it in your coat pocket and look sweet and innocent when you pay at the cashier's."

"I don't think so—," Liz started to say, but Heidi broke in.

"Come on. I'd do it myself, but I left my coat in the car."

Liz hesitated. She was tempted to do it, just to prove to Heidi that she could be daring, too.

"Don't be such a goody-two-shoes coward. Sometimes I don't know why I'm friends with you. You can be so boring!" Heidi said.

Liz bit her lip. Those words hurt. Maybe she was boring. Maybe she was a coward. But her stomach was in a nervous knot, and she knew she'd never make it out the door with the candy bar in her pocket. Plus she knew it was wrong.

"I'm sorry. I can't," she said quietly.

"Fine. Be that way." Heidi gave her a disgusted look, then turned and hurried out of sight.

Bullies don't always call you names or threaten physical violence. Sometimes they come in the form of "friends" who want something from you and threaten to embarrass you or tell you you're not cool if you refuse.

It's possible that Heidi won't want to be friends with Liz anymore. It's possible that Heidi will try to turn people at school against Liz, by telling them she's dull and boring or by claiming that Liz doesn't know how to have a little fun. Heidi might even twist this situation around and tell others that Liz can't be counted on to do even a simple favor for a friend.

If Heidi chooses to behave this way, there's really nothing Liz can do about it. All Liz can do is be herself. There will be people who will appreciate her honesty and her commitment to doing what's right and who will continue to be her friends. These are also people who will most likely recognize Heidi for the bully that she is.

Liz trusted her instincts, which told her that following Heidi's suggestion was wrong. She stood her ground, even when Heidi's words hurt her feelings. Liz remembered what was important: being true to herself. She should feel proud of her decision.

Heidi was actually the coward in this situation, because she wanted Liz to take all the risks for her. Bullies are like that. But by refusing to do what Heidi wanted her to do, Liz avoided getting into trouble and having to live with a guilty conscience.

Standing Up to Groups

Anne was so hungry! As she stood in the lunch line, the smell of french fries was almost too much. She wished the line would move a little faster.

Suddenly Selena and Tanya walked up and joined Diane, who was in line just in front of Anne. They squeezed in and started chatting. Anne was stunned.

"Excuse me," Anne said, "but you just cut in front of me."

The three girls turned and stared at Anne. "I was saving their places," Diane explained.

Anne looked at the girls. She could tell they were silently daring her to say anything more. She suddenly felt very alone. She took a deep breath. "We're not allowed to save places in the lunch line."

"Oh, come on, the three of us want to eat together. And it's not like they're going to run out of food or something," Tanya said. Diane and Selena laughed at her little joke.

"It has to do with being fair," Anne said. She was feeling very self-conscious, and her cheeks felt warm. She knew she was blushing. "You cut in front of other people who've been waiting longer."

"Please. You're only going to wait one minute longer. I can't believe you're making such a big deal out of this." Diane looked at her friends and rolled her eyes, as if to say, Is this girl a jerk or what?

Anne was feeling less and less comfortable with this. She felt outnumbered. "Okay, never mind," she said, as she took a step back to allow more room for the three girls ahead of her.

Anne had a right to challenge the girls who were breaking in line. They were not being fair to her or to the others in line behind her. Anne also had the right to give up the challenge when she felt uncomfortable. It was three against one, and no one likes those odds. But now the three girls know that Anne is an easy target. They know that if they confront her together, she will probably back down.

Anne could have spoken loudly, so that others around her would have been aware of what was happening. The more she called attention to the girls breaking in line, the more they might have been uncomfortable. Have you ever broken in line? Didn't you know you were doing something wrong and hoped that no one would say anything about it?

If you had been in line behind Anne, what would you have done? Would you have spoken up? Or would you have watched Anne handle it, hoping she would take the risk of standing up to the girls without your having to get involved? And when Anne backed down, how would you feel? Would you be glad that you hadn't done anything?

Bullies like to isolate people. They like to make you feel that you're all alone and helpless. Haven't you felt that way when picked on by a bully? And haven't you wished that someone else would help you out? If only two more people had backed Anne up, then it would have been three against three, and the girls probably would have backed down.

It's scary to step into the middle when you can simply watch from the sidelines. But coming to the aid of others who are being victimized by bullies sends a very clear message: If they pick on your friends, they're going to have to deal with you, too. And vice versa: If they pick on you, they're going to have to deal with your friends. That's what the Three Musketeers mean when they say, "All for one, one for all."

How can you be sure that others will come to your aid when you need it? You can't. But by standing up for them first, you can show them how it works. You can let the bullies know that you're not going to abandon one another to face them alone. A word of advice: Use caution if helping someone means you're likely to get injured yourself.

Dealing with Bullies Who Threaten You with Physical Violence
"Hey, Four Eyes! Where ya going so fast?"

Arnie tried to pretend he hadn't heard anything and kept walking.

"Hey, you little wimp, I'm talking to you." Brian swerved his bike in front of Arnie and came to a skidding stop. "Are you ignoring me?"

It was the first day of school, and so far fifth grade was start-ing out like all the others. Arnie was smart—very smart—and for some reason this really bothered Brian. Arnie was thin and wore glasses, and Brian constantly teased him about his looks.

"Yeah, I think you were trying to ignore me," Brian said. "That's not allowed."

Arnie felt his heart start beating wildly, especially when he saw Matt and Luis pull up on their bikes. They were Brian's cheering section and followed him everywhere.

"Sorry, I was thinking of something else. I didn't hear you," Arnie said.

"Really." Brian got off his bike and stood right in front of Arnie. "Can you hear me now?"

"Yeah," Arnie said. He tried to look Brian in the eye but found himself looking at the ground instead.

"You know, I forgot how much I hate the sight of your nerdy little face. Maybe I should rearrange it so it looks better," Brian said. Matt and Luis laughed.

Yikes! This is probably everyone's worst nightmare when it comes to bullies. You're alone, you're outnumbered, and they're threatening you with violence, which they probably plan to carry out. What can you do?

First, you can de-escalate the situation, which we know means to calm things down, to try to talk your way out. The opposite of this would be to escalate a situation, or to make things worse.

For example, if Arnie were to start calling Brian names ("Okay, fathead, just try to rearrange my face!"), he would be escalating the situation. Brian would probably come back with another insult ("Why, you stupid little jerk"), and the fight would be on.

Or Arnie could de-escalate by talking calmly and agreeing with Brian ("You don't have to rearrange my face. I'll just leave, and then you won't have to look at me anymore."). Or he could say, "Brian, I know you're stronger than I am, so we don't have to fight." Bullies like to throw out insults as bait. They want you to take the bait and escalate the situation, possibly getting you involved in a fight. One option is not to play their game.

Remember, words cannot hurt you. Bullies will use words to intimidate you, to embarrass you, or to draw you into a fight. They'll insult you or your friends and family in order to make you angry and upset and scared. Don't fall into their trap. The fastest way to take the air out of their balloon is to agree with them. It leaves them with nowhere to go.

Sometimes, of course, you can't talk your way out of a situation. Sometimes you may have to fight to defend yourself. Read Chapter Nine for some tips on how to fight. But remember, this is always your last option.

In this situation Arnie might have to fight. Brian has his two friends with him, and he may not want them to see him back down from a fight. But Arnie will probably have to fight only Brian. If their leader loses, the others may lose their confidence and start thinking about how to get out fast. Remember, bullies are cowards, and they are acting as a group. Matt and Luis follow Brian for a reason: They like pretending to be tough, but they don't really want to prove it. They don't want to get in a fight at all. They'd rather have Brian do the fighting for them.

If Brian wins this fight, Matt and Luis will slap him on the back and throw some insults at Arnie, but that will be it. If Arnie wins the fight, they may pick Brian up and drag him away, still throwing insults at

Arnie. But they probably won't challenge someone who just beat their leader.

This is a good time for Arnie to draw on his self-esteem. It's hard to conjure up self-esteem on the spot. That's why it's important to work on it all the time—so that it's strong when you need it. Arnie knows why he is being picked on: because he is different from Brian and his friends. But being different doesn't mean that Arnie is less of a person in any way. Being different does not make it okay for others to bully him.

Arnie is smart. He has lots of other qualities and accomplishments that he can be proud of. He needs to remember these things when a bully like Brian tries to make him feel bad. Arnie's self-esteem is part of his self-defense. Without it he'll always have a hard time standing up to bullies.

One option you always have with a bully is to inform an adult, like a teacher or parent or coach, of the bully's behavior. (See Chapter Seven—"Getting Help.") This is not a cowardly way out. No one considers a grown-up a coward if he or she calls the police when someone is disturbing the peace or making threats. Adults in positions of authority are there to help with a problem like this.

ANSWERS TO "WHAT IF...?"

What if . . . you ride the bus to school and there's a kid or group of kids who are always picking on you, calling you names, and stealing your things?

First, you can try target denial. Is there another way for you to get to and from school? Can you carpool with someone else? Can you walk or ride a bike? Is there another bus you can switch to? If you have to ride this bus, perhaps you can talk to the bus driver. Explain the situation, and then arrange to sit up front, near the driver.

Are there other kids who are also being harassed? Perhaps you can cooperate with them to sit together and provide support for one another. There is strength in numbers, and bullies don't like being outnumbered.

Remember, you have control over how you respond to the bullying. If you get upset, if you cry or beg bullies to stop, if you appear scared and intimidated, the bullying will probably continue. Instead you can ignore it. Words are just words, and nothing is more annoying than trying to bother someone who refuses to be bothered. You can use your voice, look the bullies in the eye, and boldly tell them to stop. You may be scared to death and shaking on the inside, but don't let them see it.

You can also use your voice by taking this to higher authorities. Tell your parents, your teacher, the principal, or a school counselor. They can take action that you can't, such as punishing the bullies or speaking to their parents.

What if . . . someone in your class insists that you let him or her cheat off your test and, if you don't let him or her cheat, he or she threatens not to be your friend anymore and to tell everyone your big secret?

You can give in, if you want, and let him or her cheat. But then this person will probably want to cheat off you again in the future. You've allowed it once, so why not twice? Or three times? Or for the rest of the school year? Maybe this bully would also like you to do his or her homework as well. Now that the bully has found an easy way to blackmail you, why stop with getting answers on the tests? Why not have you do even more work for him or her?

Your other option is to say no. It may mean losing the person's friendship. Well, good riddance. Friends don't threaten friends. Friends don't ask friends to lie or cheat for them. The risk here is that the person will carry through on the threat and tell your secret. You have to decide if it's worth that.

There is a warning in this "What If . . . ?" question: Be careful whom you trust with your secrets. Get to know people before you tell them things that you don't want everyone else to know. Make sure that someone is worthy of your trust. Trustworthy friends prove it by what they do, not what they say.

What if . . . a bully corners you in the locker room, picks up a baseball bat, and begins to taunt you by swinging at your knees and barely missing them?

Look around and see if you are alone or if there are other students or a teacher nearby. If there are others around you, ask for help with a loud, clear voice. If you're alone, try de-escalation: "Hey, you don't need to use the bat. . . . I was just leaving." If you can't de-escalate the situation, stand your ground and be ready to defend yourself. Tell the bully, "Stop" and mean it with your voice, body language, and eye contact. Even if you are shaking on the inside (and who wouldn't be afraid?), try to make your outside look strong, steady, and confident. Finally, make sure you report the bully's behavior to a teacher or your parent.

STAYING SAFE AT HOME

5

WHAT IF...?

What if . . . you answer the phone and someone claims to be calling from a local radio station and says you just won a big prize. But first, the station needs some information—your name and address, how old you are, what school you go to—before sending the prize.

What if . . . you're coming home from school and, as you near your house, you notice that a screen has been pulled off and the curtains are blowing out through the open window?

Even though most of us think that danger exists outside our homes—perhaps only on the streets or in the schoolyard—crime does occur in or near our homes. For most of your life your parents and other loved ones have tried to watch out for you and keep you safe, particularly at home. You have probably had some discussions with your parents regarding how to answer the telephone or when to answer the door. However, as you get older, you need to start taking more responsibility for your own safety. You may even find yourself in charge of the safety of others—for instance, when baby-sitting younger brothers and sisters.

PAY ATTENTION TO YOUR HOME ENVIRONMENT

To maximize your safety at home, pay attention to the following:

● Open windows or unlocked doors. These could be signs that someone has entered your home.

● Bushes or trees in front of your house. These are places where someone can hide to surprise you.

● Laundry rooms, parking garages, elevators, or alleyways—especially if you're alone or if these places don't have good lighting. Assailants prefer to attack victims in places like these, which are often isolated and allow the attacker an opportunity to take a victim by surprise.

● Strange people or strange vehicles (like vans) around your street or apartment complex. Tell an adult. Assailants and burglars like to "case out" people and places before choosing their targets.

Plan ahead. Your home is one place where you have some control regarding your safety. It's always a good idea to keep your doors locked, even if you live in a neighborhood that you think is safe. Especially when you go to bed at night or when you're home by yourself, all doors and windows should be closed and locked. Close any curtains and blinds after the sun goes down, so you can't be seen through the windows. If your home has a sliding glass door, talk to your parents about putting a small metal pole in the track on the floor so the door can't be opened, even if it's left unlocked. Local police departments may offer advice on how to keep your home safe.

How to Deal with Strangers at the Door

You may already be familiar with the following strategies, but it can't hurt to go over them again:

- *Never open the door for strangers.*
- Use the peephole or a window to check outside and see if you recognize the person. If there is no way to check, you can pretend you're not home or you can talk to the person through the door. Ask who it is and what he or she wants.
- Don't give out personal information.
- If you do not know the person, *do not let him or her in*!
- Let your parents know that you are not comfortable being left alone to deal with repair or service people. If someone is delivering a package, ask if the person can leave it on the doorstep or with a neighbor or can come back the next day. If it is a service person (like telephone repair or cable TV), ask him or her to show you a photo ID and to slide a business card under the door or through the mail slot or to leave it in the mailbox. Say you'll give the busi-

ness card to your parents, but *do not let that person in.* Genuine service people will understand that a child at home alone cannot let them in the house, and they won't insist on coming in.

● Don't worry about hurting people's feelings or making them come back another time. It is better for an adult to deal with these situations. Just *don't let them in.*

You Can't Come In

Scott was home on a Saturday afternoon watching a movie on television. His parents were out shopping for a new couch and would probably be gone for hours. Scott was enjoying having the house to himself.

Just as the movie got to the good part, the doorbell rang. Scott thought about ignoring it, but then a commercial came on, and he decided to find out who was ringing the bell. He went to the front hallway and double-checked that the door was locked. Since there was no peephole, Scott spoke through the door.

"Who is it?" he asked.

"I'm looking for Mr. Charles Rosado," came the answer.

"He's not available," Scott said. He was straining to see the TV in the next room so he could be sure to get in there before the movie came back on.

"That's just great. Look, I have some papers for him. Can I leave them with you?" The woman sounded upset.

Scott knew the rule: Don't open the door for strangers. He said, "No, you'll have to come back."

"Come on, kid. Just open the door and take these, okay? They're important papers." Scott could almost feel the woman's anger and frustration. He was getting nervous and wasn't sure what to do. Should he open the door and just take the papers?

He said: "I am not opening the door. Can't you just leave them in the mailbox?" This seemed reasonable to Scott; he could get them after he saw the woman go away.

This time the woman got very angry, began to bang the door, and demanded that Scott open the door.

What could Scott have done? He was in an awkward and uncomfortable position. He was alone in the house, and this person was insisting that he open the door. Even though Scott knew the rule, he hesitated to enforce it; he wanted to help the woman. It seemed easy enough to open the door and take the papers. Saying no can be difficult. What might happen if Scott did agree to open the door? Well, he would be home alone with a stranger who would no longer be at a safe distance! From a safety perspective, that's not a good idea. Those papers are not worth his being put into such a vulnerable position.

Scott understood that the rule about not opening the door for strangers is important. It is the best way to keep him safe when he is home alone. It is not his responsibility to help a stranger or fix her problem. Telling the stranger to leave the papers in the mailbox was a clever solution. Another option might have been to send the woman to a neighbor's home and have her leave the papers there. Scott did not let the stranger bully him into forgetting or breaking the rule.

If Someone Tries to Get into Your Home

You probably feel comfortable and familiar with the rules about what to do if someone knocks at the door and you are home alone. However, you may be more afraid of a situation where a criminal is forcing his or her way into your home. So if you suspect someone has broken into or is breaking into your house, follow these steps:

● If you come home and it looks as if there's been a break-in, don't go in the house. The person may still be there! Leave immediately and go to a neighbor's or some other safe place to call the police.

● If you are inside your house and hear someone breaking in, again, leave immediately. If you can't get away, lock yourself in a room (such as a bedroom) with a telephone and dial 911. Speak slowly and clearly so the operator can understand you. Give your full name and address and tell the operator where you are in the house and what's happening. If you can, stay on the phone and tell the operator what is going on until help arrives.

● If you don't think that you can stay on the phone, dial 911 and *don't hang up.* Hide the phone under a bed or someplace else where it will be out of sight. In many cities, if there is no answer at your end of the phone after you've called 911, the emergency operator will automatically send the police to check on the situation. Then find a place to hide—under a bed, for instance, or in the back of a closet—or lock yourself in a room.

● If you are in a locked room, you can yell out to the intruder that you know he or she is there and that you've called the police, who are on their way. This could be enough to scare an intruder into leaving.

Here are some other ways you can plan ahead to help keep your home safe:

● Make sure you have emergency numbers handy. If 911 service is not available in your area, ask your parents or an operator what number you should call in an emergency. Use this number only for emergencies. Keep other important telephone numbers—for the police, the fire department, your parents at work, and neighbors or relatives that you can call—next to the telephone, in large, easy-to-read figures. Go over with your parents the best people to call in different types of emergencies.

● Ask your parents to give a trusted neighbor a set of keys to your home. Don't keep an extra set under a flower pot or doormat; thieves know all the usual hiding places for keys!

● Set up a plan with your parents so that they will always know where to find you should you ever get separated from them or should you need to find a safe place other than home. This safe haven can be your school or a neighbor's house, anyplace where you can get help and shelter.

● Agree on a code word with your parents, something they can yell to you in an emergency (a fire, an earthquake, an intruder in the house), that lets you know you need to get out of the house and go to the safe haven.

● Make sure you know how to open, close, lock, and unlock all the windows and doors in your home.

DEALING WITH STRANGERS ON THE PHONE

Sometimes criminals will use the telephone to find out if you are alone. You may know some of the following tips regarding telephone use, but again, it doesn't hurt to go over them to be sure.

● If you have an answering machine, let it pick up and take a message when you're home alone.

● Never give out such personal information as your name, your address, or your telephone number.

● If someone calls your number by mistake, ask what number he or she was trying to reach. Tell the caller he or she has reached the wrong number, but do not give out your number and do not confirm your number.

● Never tell someone that you are home alone. Tell the caller that your parents can't come to the phone at the moment and they've asked you to take a message. Write down the caller's name and phone number and tell the person your parents will call back shortly.

● If you ever feel uncomfortable with people on the phone—if their questions are personal, if they begin making sexual references—hang up. If they call back, hang up again, or let the answering machine pick up.

● If an obscene phone caller keeps calling back, you can blow a whistle—really loudly—into the telephone mouthpiece.

● If a problem with an obscene caller continues, keep a log of the calls, noting the day and time of each call. (This can help the police catch the caller.) Notify the telephone company, the police, and, of course, your parents.

Some areas of the country have an automatic call-back feature or the ability to block certain people from calling you. As better technology arrives, you may have other options. Talk to your parents about what's available where you live and what you can use in your home.

SAFETY ON THE INTERNET

Since you log on to the Internet through a telephone line, the same safety rules for telephone use apply here. You may want to post the following guidelines near your computer, so you can remember them when you're on-line:

● Never give out your name, your address, your telephone number, or the name of your school on-line. It may be safe to tell people your city or state, but check with your parents about exactly what information they think is okay to give out.

● If you post anything on a message board, read your message carefully before posting it. Double-check to be sure that you're not giving out any personal information.

● Keep your password for getting on-line a secret. Do not tell anyone, not even your best friend, your password for any reason. Genuine representatives of on-line servers—such as America Online—will *never* ask for your password. So don't be fooled by someone who asks for your password, claiming to be an official with your on-line service. That person is not telling the truth.

● If you're uncomfortable with what someone on-line has said to you, or if you feel threatened by someone on-line, leave that chat room or sign off. If you can, write down the person's screen name and tell your parents or an on-line representative. They may want to alert other authorities, and giving them the screen name can help.

● Never agree to meet someone in person without asking a parent first and telling that parent that you met this person on-line.

● Remember, when you're on-line, you can't see the people you're communicating with, so it's hard to know if they are being honest about themselves. That's why it's particularly important to be careful in dealing with the people you meet on the Internet.

Don't Give Out Any Information on the Telephone

Meghan ran to answer the ringing telephone before the answering machine picked up. "Hello, Davis residence," she said, a little out of breath.

"Well, hi. Umm, I'm calling for your mom. Is she home?" a man's voice asked.

"Yes, she's outside. I'll go get her," Meghan answered.

"No, no, that's okay. Don't bother her if she's busy. Maybe you can just take a message for me."

"Okay, sure." Meghan saw the family message pad, but as usual, there was no pencil in sight. "Just let me find something to write with."

"Fine. There's no hurry. You know, I forget how old your mom told me you are. What grade are you in now?" the man asked. He sounded nice; his voice was casual.

She answered that she was in fifth grade and said, "I found a pencil."

"My name is William. Your mom knows me. What's your name? I apologize that I don't remember. I know your mother told me, but I'm really bad with names."

All of a sudden Meghan felt a tightening in her stomach. She realized that this man was getting a lot of information about her, and she didn't remember her mother ever mentioning anyone named William.

She decided that she needed to end the phone call. She pretended that her mother was walking in the door and said, "I think I hear my mom coming in the back door. Hold on and I'll get her for you."

"Oops, that's my call waiting. I'll have to call her back," William said, and quickly hung up.

Meghan was smart to listen to her gut. As soon as she realized that she was being "interviewed" by the caller, she stopped giving out any more personal information. Did you notice that Meghan was tricked into giving out her grade in school? She was right to be polite on the phone (there is no need to be rude), but she also needed to remember the telephone rules.

Meghan did not reveal that she was alone in the house and came up with a clever strategy to "test" the caller by saying that her mom was coming in the door. If the person had really wanted to speak with Meghan's mother, he would have stayed on the telephone until she picked up. Meghan had other options as well. She could have quickly taken his name and number, or she could have hung up.

ANSWERS TO "WHAT IF...?"

What if . . . you answer the phone and someone claims to be calling from a local radio station and says you just won a big prize. But first, the station needs some information—your name and address, how old you are, what school you go to—before sending the prize.

Don't give out any personal information, even if it seems that you may be winning a prize. Ask to take the person's name and telephone number, and ask what organization he or she is calling from. Have a parent call the number back; perhaps you did win a big prize. Don't let the person pressure you into giving out any information by claiming that time is running out and you have to respond immediately. Don't forget to listen to your gut. If it sounds too good to be true, it probably is.

What if . . . you're coming home from school and, as you near your house, you notice that a screen has been pulled off and the curtains are blowing out through the open window?

Do not go into the house under any circumstances. Immediately go to a neighbor's home or a store and call 911. Tell the police who you are and where you are calling from. It is likely that your home has been burglarized, and going into the house to check things out could be extremely dangerous if the criminals are still there. This is an adult problem that needs adult attention.

Pay attention to any signs that things have been disturbed. Open windows, missing screens, open or unlocked doors are indications that someone has forced his or her way into your home. If you come home and see evidence of a search, like drawers pulled open or your things scattered around, or if you notice valuables missing, leave immediately and go to a safe place. Notify an adult right away, and let the police know what happened, too.

SAFETY AWAY FROM HOME

WHAT IF...?

What if . . . you're at soccer practice, and you see a strange man watching from across the street. This is the third time you've seen him there, and none of the other kids knows who he is.

What if . . . you see a flasher (someone who is exposing his or her private parts)?

What if . . . you are walking home from school and you notice a person following you?

There are many different circumstances you may find yourself in away from home. We'll cover a few of them here, but the main thing you need to remember is what we talked about in earlier chapters. Remember the basics!

TARGET DENIAL

● Be careful of shortcuts that will take you through deserted areas, empty lots, or alleyways. Be extra alert in shopping center parking lots, and stay away from vans in particular.

● Whenever possible, go out with other people. One kid alone is a much easier target than two or more kids together.

● Avoid groups of older kids. Often kids will behave worse when they're with their friends than they would if you met them alone. Also, a group of kids could be gang members.

BE AWARE

● If you have to wait somewhere for a ride to pick you up, stay alert. Don't bury your head in a book or magazine, because then you won't notice what's going on around you. Pay attention to the people near you (remember the two arm's lengths rule) and to the cars passing by. Think about what you could do if you had to escape someone who was threatening you. Where are the safe places you could run to; what direction would you go; are there other people nearby who would hear if you started yelling?

● If you think you're being followed, turn around to see who's behind you. This might scare someone away, because now you've "caught" the person in the act. If you still think someone is following you, cross the street, or go into a store where you can use a phone to call your parents or the police. Whenever possible, go where there are other people. If you find yourself alone, running is always an option, especially if the other person is getting closer. If you're carrying things that interfere with your running—backpacks, skateboards, books—drop them and leave them behind. Your safety is more important!

● Kidnappings frequently happen in parking lots, and vans are often used in abductions. Look around; make it difficult for someone to sneak up on you.

● Use your peripheral vision to keep an eye on people around you (remember the exercise in Chapter One where you held out your arms and saw your wiggling fingers out of the corners of your eyes?). You can also use reflections in store windows or car windows to check on who's behind you.

PLAN AHEAD

● If you're being dropped off at a mall or store, make sure you are dropped off and picked up in a well-lit area with other people around.

● If you are carrying more than twenty dollars in cash on you, divide it up among different pockets and a purse or wallet. Pull out only what you need (to buy a movie ticket, or gum or candy, or a magazine or comic book). Be careful not to make it obvious how much money you have, because someone who notices may decide to take it from you.

● Have enough money with you to be able to call for help or a ride. Know whom to call, and either memorize the number(s) or keep them with you all the time.

LISTEN TO YOUR GUT

If something makes you uncomfortable, pay attention to the feeling.

Don't be afraid to leave or walk away. Trust your instincts. For example, public bathrooms (like those at movie theaters, beaches and parks, schools, and shopping malls) can be dangerous places. If you walk into a bathroom and you get a bad feeling about a person or people inside, leave immediately. Here are some safety strategies:

- Choose the stall nearest the exit door.
- Be alert to how many other people are in the bathroom.
- Whenever possible, have a friend or family member go with you, or have someone wait just outside the bathroom for you.
- Place your packages or other valuables (knapsack, purse, wallet) at the back of the stall so it is harder for anyone to grab them.
- If you see a flasher, walk away as quickly as possible, and tell an adult you trust. You may want to call the police and give them a description of the flasher.

USE YOUR VOICE

If you see a crime being committed, go get help: Call 911, or find an adult who you think can assist. If possible, remember everything you can about the person committing the crime, such as age, size, and skin color, if he has a beard or mustache, what color clothes the person is wearing, if he or she has a jacket or coat, what kind of shoes the criminal has on, and so on. The victim will probably be experiencing the freeze response and will be too scared to remember what the assailant looked like. Your description can be a great help to the police.

Street-Smart Skills

"Yes!" Johnny screamed as he and his bicycle landed safely on the pavement.

As Johnny took a lap around the empty church parking lot, he noticed a car parked on the other side of the lot. He wasn't certain how long it had been there; he'd been so caught up in practicing jumps with his bicycle that he hadn't paid much attention to anything else around him. There was a man in the car who appeared to be looking in Johnny's direction, but it was hard to tell because of the reflections on the car window.

After Johnny again sailed off the ramp and came down in one piece, he made a wide curve around the parking lot. The man had rolled down his window and was waving at him.

"Excuse me, young man. Could you help me?" He smiled and looked apologetic. "I seem to be a little lost."

Johnny glanced around. The parking lot was deserted. Johnny figured that as long as the man remained in the car and Johnny had his bicycle, it was okay to help. He rode his bike closer to the man's car.

"I have an address written down here—could you take a look at it?" The man held up a piece of paper with some writing on it.

"Sure," Johnny said, and he rode up to the car. As he got nearer, the man lowered the piece of paper to his lap. Johnny thought this was odd, especially if the man wanted him to read the numbers. Once he reached the window, he looked in the

car, and he froze. The man wasn't wearing any pants! Johnny could see—well, everything!

The man had a strange expression on his face, and he was just staring at Johnny. Johnny felt the hairs on the back of his neck stand up. His mind was screaming, Go, run, move! and finally, with great effort, his body started to respond. He frantically turned around, got his legs pumping, and flew across the parking lot on the bicycle. When he reached the sidewalk, he glanced over his shoulder and saw the car starting to move. At first he thought the man was coming after him, but then he saw the car make a U-turn in the parking lot and drive off in the opposite direction.

Did you realize, as you were reading, that it would have been safer for Johnny to leave the parking lot and ride home rather than practice so close to a parked car with a stranger in it? We all know what it is like to be lost and how grateful we are when someone points us in the right direction. But even though Johnny was just trying to be helpful, his behavior placed him in some danger. Getting within two arm's lengths was a violation of the safety rules and put him at risk. Johnny shouldn't be so close to the car that the driver can reach out and grab his arm.

What clues did Johnny get early on to let him know this person wasn't really lost? First, Johnny noticed the parked car and thought he was being watched. Most people who are lost drive around and look for a gas station or someone in a uniform to help them with directions. Second, the man lowered the paper toward his lap. How could Johnny read the paper if it was in his lap? Both these clues should alert you to the fact that something is wrong. Your gut should be saying uh-oh. Awareness doesn't just mean looking around you; it also means paying attention to what is going on right in front of you!

What's more, an adult should not be asking a child for directions. Johnny would have been better off leaving the parking lot for a more populated area or directing the man to an adult who could help. Also, if Johnny had been more aware and noticed how long the car had been parked there, he might have been more suspicious of the driver. He might not have responded to the driver's request for help or gotten so close to the car.

If a vehicle slows down as it comes near you, keep a lot of distance between you and it. Look for the nearest safe place or turn around and go in the opposite direction from the vehicle. If the occupants of the vehicle are strangers to you, you do not have to respond if they call out to you. You do not have to answer their questions. And do *not*—under any circumstances—go near the vehicle!

Trust Your Instincts

Pamela and her mother had picked up some notebooks at the mall that Pamela needed for a school project. It was about 6:00 P.M., and the sun was going down. Both Pamela and her mom were tired and couldn't wait to get home and eat dinner. As they walked through the parking lot, Pamela was in her own little world, thinking about her schoolwork. Suddenly she noticed something out of the corner of her eye. But they were in such a rush that she did not want to bother her mother with her paranoia.

They were almost at the car when Pamela felt a presence. Instead of second-guessing herself, she took her mother's arm and pulled her into the center of the parking lot away from the cars and headed back to the stores. Her mother shook off Pamela's grip and said, "What are you doing? We're in a hurry!"

Pamela's actions show she had a heightened sense of awareness. She really listened to her gut and took quick action. Walking toward your car in a mall is an excellent time to practice your awareness and target denial skills, even if you are tired and hungry. Shopping centers are places that criminals frequent, because they know people have money or newly bought possessions. Also, the parking lots at shopping areas can be poorly lit and far away from the stores and the majority of shoppers.

What would have happened if Pamela hadn't listened to her gut and had paid no attention to warning signs? Well, it is possible that nothing would have happened. Maybe there really was no danger. On the other hand, someone could have been trying to sneak up on them without being seen or heard. By the time Pamela had seen or heard that person again, he or she might have been closer than a safe distance.

Even if you think you are being nervous for no reason, it is best to walk away from potential danger. Pamela's mother may have thought her daughter was overreacting to shadows moving, but

Pamela thought it was better to be safe than sorry. She decided that walking a little farther was worth the extra time it took.

SAFETY IN YOUR CAR

Cars can feel like safe havens. You're in your own little world, maybe with the radio on, rolling down the highway. It's air-conditioned relief from summer heat or a warm and cozy escape from a snowy winter. Since you don't drive yet, you can just relax and watch the scenery or pick a fight with your brothers or sisters and drive your parents crazy.

But even though you're not sitting in the driver's seat, there are some things you can do to increase your safety in a car and the safety of others with you.

- Wear your seat belt.
- Keep the doors locked and the windows up while you're in a car. If you have to be left alone in a car for any reason, check the doors and windows yourself. If someone tries to bother you while you're in the car, honk the horn and keep honking!
- You can help the driver by being alert. Point out any suspicious people you see, especially anyone who appears to be approaching the car when it's stopped.
- Before opening the car door to get out, look all around. Be aware of strangers who may be near enough to get into your car once you have opened the door.
- Look around as you approach your car to get in. Notice if anyone seems to be following you or is close enough to jump in once you have opened the door.

● What if you find yourself in a carjacking, where someone is forcing the driver to hand over the keys to the car? If you're outside the car, move away from the car as quickly as possible. Most of the time the carjacker only wants the automobile, and the easier you make it for him or her to get away with the car, the better. If you are inside the car, quickly undo your seat belt and get out of the car on the side farthest from the carjacker.

SAFETY AT SCHOOL

Your school officials do their best to make school a safe place for kids. Some schools have better funding and resources for this than others.

You can help improve your safety and that of your friends by practicing some of the following tips:

● Report any suspicious person you see hanging around your school or playground to a teacher or the principal. Keep your distance from the person, and let the adults at your school handle the situation.

● Don't accept drugs or alcohol from anyone, even if they are free. You'll probably get expelled from school, and you could be arrested. Drugs and alcohol also interfere with your ability to take care of yourself, because they slow down your responses and make you confused.

● Be alert in bathrooms. In some schools, these are the favorite hangouts of kids dealing drugs and of other types of assailants. Think about it: If an attacker locks the door, it's difficult to hear someone inside yelling for help. Whenever possible, have a friend accompany you. If you think that something is wrong, leave immediately.

● Have a code word between you and your parents (or caregivers), something that only they know. If your parents ever have to send someone else to pick you up (at school or anyplace), they should tell that person the code word. You should *never go* with someone who doesn't know the code word.

● *Never* get into a vehicle with someone you don't know!

Don't Go Anywhere with a Stranger

Perry walked out of school on a cold, snowy day. He did not see his dad's car anywhere in sight. He was pretty sure his dad had said he would pick him up. Maybe he was just a little late.

Just as he was about to go into the school and call, he saw a woman walking toward him. She said, "Hi, Perry. I work with your dad at Comtech, and he said to pick you up from school because he needs to work late." Perry was relieved he wouldn't have to wait outside any longer. It was really cold, and getting into a warm car sounded great. She told him there was a cup of hot chocolate in the car because his dad was sorry he couldn't make it. Perry said, "Okay, let me call my dad first." The woman replied that he did not need to call because his dad was really busy and she had just spoken to him.

What should Perry do? Did you notice any warning signs? We have repeated it over and over again: Don't go anywhere with a stranger. Even though this woman knew Perry's name and where his dad worked, that is not good enough. We suggest using a code word that only you and your family know as a way to figure out if you should take a ride with a stranger. Perry did not know this woman, and she did not use the code word that he and his dad had agreed on. Even though she used his name, there are many ways she could have learned it.

Another warning sign is that she discouraged him from calling his dad. It makes perfect sense that Perry would want to speak with his father before getting into a car with a stranger. The woman was also trying to bribe him with the warmth of the car and the hot chocolate. It sounded too good to be true, and it probably was.

SAFETY ON PUBLIC TRANSPORTATION

Some of you won't be riding public transportation by yourselves until you are older. Eventually most of you will have to use public transportation, even if you haven't yet. Many of you may already be riding a bus or train to get to school or around your neighborhood. So, for the times when you are alone, the following safety tips should serve you well:

● Stay aware while waiting at a bus stop or on a street corner for your transportation. Don't bury your head in a book or zone out listening to headphones; you won't notice someone approaching you until it's too late. Remember to keep two arm's lengths between yourself and strangers whenever possible.

● Sit near the front of the bus, close to the driver, or near the conductor on a train.

● Pay attention as you travel so you don't miss your stop. If you miss your stop, you may have to walk alone or wait in an unfamiliar neighborhood for another bus.

● If you're traveling with friends or family and you get separated from them, look for a person in authority (a police officer or security guard) to ask for help. Stay in public areas, where there are other people around, while you try to locate your friends or family.

Setting Boundaries on Public Transportation

Rolanda was so excited. She had made the running team organized by an incredible coach. Rolanda was only eleven, but she knew she was good, and high school coaches were already interested in her.

Practices were held two towns over from where she lived, and she and her parents decided that she would have to take the bus. Rolanda was so happy that she did not mind the inconvenience.

Rolanda liked to sit at the back of the bus, because she always got a seat and could read her magazines. One day a guy sat down right next to her in the last available seat. He smelled from drinking and kept trying to talk to her. She ignored him and went back to reading her magazines. Soon he fell asleep, leaned his head on her shoulder, and began to drool. Ugh! She was nauseated and did not know what to do.

She moved her shoulder to try to wake him up, but he was out cold. She decided just to grin and bear it and waited until her stop to get off.

Remember boundary setting from Chapter Two? This is a perfect opportunity for Rolanda to practice setting a good boundary. There was no reason for her to be uncomfortable on the bus ride or to put up with someone drooling on her shoulder. When he began to talk to her, she could have used her voice and set a boundary, saying something like "I don't want to talk to you. Leave me alone." She should not have to wait until her stop to get up and move.

Rolanda should have moved away once she decided that she didn't want to be near the man. She could also have told the driver that the man was bothering her, so the driver would pay extra attention to the situation. If she felt very threatened and the driver didn't or couldn't help her, she could get off the bus before her regular stop. It would be a good idea for her to check with the driver or another passenger to figure out which stop was the safest place to wait for the next bus.

WHAT IF YOU'RE LOST?

Have you ever gotten separated from your family or friends in a store, at a mall, or at an amusement park? It can be a very scary feeling, especially if it's a strange place. Share the following tips with your parents, brothers and sisters, and friends. That way you all will know what to do if someone gets lost, and you'll have a better chance of finding one another when it happens.

- Stay in a public area, with lots of other people around.
- Practice all your skills: awareness, keeping your distance, listening to your gut.

● If it's safe, stay close to the spot where you last saw your family or friends. That's probably the first place they'll look for you.

● Locate a police officer, security guard, salesperson, or someone in charge, and tell him or her what happened. He or she may be able to page your companions and tell them where you are.

● If a security guard or any other person in charge suggests going to an office or some other waiting area, tell him or her you would rather wait in a public area. Remember, this person—even though he or she may be a security guard or police officer—is a stranger to you. It's best to stay where there are other people around and to avoid being alone with someone you don't know.

A WORD (OR TWO) ABOUT ALCOHOL AND DRUGS

You've probably heard lots of warnings against alcohol and drugs. Well, here's one more: Your safety is your responsibility. When you're drunk or high, you cannot take care of yourself. You're not thinking clearly, your body moves more slowly, and you are more likely to do things that you would never do if you were sober. Many times assailants are under the influence of alcohol or drugs when they commit their crimes. You become an easier target for them when you're also drunk or high.

The choice is yours, but remember, it is a choice. You can say no, or you can say yes. If you say yes to alcohol or drugs, be aware that you may be putting yourself in danger.

ANSWERS TO "WHAT IF...?"

What if . . . you're at soccer practice, and you see a strange man watching from across the street. This is the third time you've seen him there, and none of the other kids knows who he is.

Walk away, go to a public place, and immediately report this to an adult. It could be a harmless person who just enjoys watching soccer, but it is not your responsibility to find out. Assailants sometimes hang out where there are lots of children, looking for potential victims. An adult should investigate. Don't pretend that he is not there or that this is not a problem. That is not good personal safety. You may be putting yourself and your teammates at risk.

What if . . . you see a flasher (someone who is exposing his or her private parts)?

You may giggle as you read this, but it happens. Most of the time flashers are doing this just to see the shock on your face. It is important that you are not so shocked by this incident that you can't move away or get to safety. Take a deep breath, look around, and move as quickly as you can to a safe place. We encourage you to tell a parent or teacher. You may also want to call the police and give them a description of the person. Even though flashers are rarely dangerous, it would be a good idea to move to a safe place before writing down a description.

What if . . . you are walking home from school and you notice a person following you?

Immediately walk toward a safe place while keeping your eye on the person. A safe place may be a store or a friend's home. Get to the closest safe place you can find. If you are far from a safe place, cross the street, and walk back toward school or a more populated area. The idea is to get to a place where you can find help and other people: a restaurant, a convenience store, a police station, or a gas station.

GETTING HELP

7

What if . . . someone says that he or she wants to take photographs of you for a magazine or a modeling agency but that you can't tell your parents?

What if . . . your brother's friend offers you a hundred dollars to deliver an envelope but makes you promise not to tell anyone?

What if . . . you think a neighbor is watching you through your bedroom window while you get undressed at night?

Throughout this book we've tried to show you that you can take responsibility for your own safety. You can learn how to be aware, how to identify potential dangers, how to walk away from danger, and how to think through challenging problems. We've also encouraged you to tell a parent or trusted adult when you're in trouble. Asking for help is sometimes necessary, because we can't always solve problems on our own.

WE ALL NEED HELP SOMETIMES

Everyone needs help at one time or another. It is a sign of wisdom and maturity to know when a situation is too difficult for you to deal with on your own. Even the president of the United States is surrounded by people he can call on for help.

There's a saying "Two heads are better than one," and it's very true. One person may be so caught up in his or her problem that the person can't see a way out, but someone looking at the situation from the outside may be able to see a number of solutions. Have you noticed that this book has two authors? That's because we realized that the final product would be better if we put our heads together and worked as a team.

You can ask adults for help in all kinds of situations. They can help with things like homework and clothes shopping. They can also help in situations that are more challenging, like when a bully will not stop bothering you and when an adult (or teenager) is sexually inappropriate and/or threatening you.

Getting Help for Problems with Other Kids
Miranda was walking to school, going over the questions that she knew were going to be on her history quiz that morning.

She didn't notice the two junior high boys until they were right in front of her and she had nearly bumped into them.

"Sorry. Excuse me," Miranda said as she tried to walk around them.

"Hey, kid. Don't you know that this is a toll sidewalk?" one of the boys said.

"What?" Miranda didn't understand the question. She'd never seen these two boys before.

"I said, this is a toll sidewalk. You gotta pay us the toll before you can go any farther." The boy was standing directly in her path, holding out one hand. His friend was standing slightly behind him, glancing around to make sure no one else was watching.

Miranda started to get scared. "I don't have any money on me," she said softly. She could feel her throat closing up and tears welling in her eyes. She just wanted to get to school and be left alone.

"Well, then, you've got a problem," the boy answered, and took a step closer. "But I'm in a good mood today. Maybe we'll be willing to take something else instead. What have you got?"

Miranda was having a hard time thinking clearly. She wasn't wearing any jewelry, just a watch. She took it off and silently held it out to the boy. He looked at it and frowned.

"Well, if this is all you've got, it will have to do. Tomorrow make sure you bring some money, okay? And don't tell anyone about this. We know where to find you." The boy and his friend quickly ran away.

Miranda's body was shaking. She was terrified. And she had given them her watch, which was a gift from her grandmother! Her parents were going to be furious with her. Slowly she placed one foot in front of the other, forcing herself to continue walking toward school, keeping an eye out for those boys and wiping away the tears as she went.

The next day she tried walking to school from a different direction. The same boys were waiting for her when she got to the door. She told them she did not have any money and this time decided to hold her ground and say, "Just leave me alone. You have my watch; I don't have anything else." She kept her eye on them and ran into the school. She'd gotten through the ordeal today, but what was she going to do tomorrow? And the day after that? Why were they picking on her?

This time she decided to tell a teacher what happened. Together they went to the principal's office, and the principal assured Miranda he would do something about the boys. In the meantime he suggested that she walk to school with a friend or get one of her parents to walk with her. Miranda hadn't even thought of "safety in numbers."

Miranda tried at first to handle the problem on her own. She did a pretty good job the first day she was approached by the bullies. It was wise of her to offer the boys her watch when she didn't have any money. Things can be replaced, but *you* can't. However, that solution won't work if they keep coming back; you don't want to have to "pay the toll" every day. Did you notice that Miranda was distracted and didn't notice the bullies soon enough to avoid them? Target denial might have helped her avoid the situation completely.

By the time the bullies approached her the second time, Miranda had chosen another option: holding her ground. This may work. Sometimes bullies are looking for kids who are easy to overwhelm and intimidate. If Miranda uses her voice and demonstrates that she is not an easy target (or will not be an easy target again), they may go away. If the bullying persists, it is time to seek help.

Believe it or not, every adult was at one time your age. And each one also experienced peer pressure, had to deal with bullies, and felt insecure and confused. Having been through this themselves, adults may have solutions you haven't thought of.

GETTING HELP WITH UNWANTED TOUCH

In the case of unwanted touch or sexual harassment, it is especially important that you inform a trusted adult and let him or her take charge. If you have been assaulted, you need to tell an adult so he or she can make certain you get the help you need. You may have to see a doctor to take care of any physical injuries and a counselor who can help you deal with your feelings about the assault. If it becomes necessary for you to visit a doctor and counselor, be honest with them. They can help you better if they know everything that has happened to you.

Sometimes it is hard to find an adult whom you can confide in. You may not be sure that anyone will believe you. You may be afraid that the adult will blame you for what has happened or think

that you did something wrong. Just remember, it's not your fault. No one has the right to hurt you or make you uncomfortable. Even though it may be hard to tell someone what has happened to you, it is critical that you do so. The following are guidelines for how to get adult help:

● Insist that the adult you are confiding in stop whatever else he or she may be doing and give you his or her complete attention. Do not try to tell adults what happened while they're on the phone, talking to other people, or trying to get out the door. What happened to you requires their undivided attention.

● Start at the beginning. Tell what happened in the order that it happened. Don't leave anything out. Even if you think that you said or did something that contributed to the incident, tell everything. This will help the adult you're confiding in understand, and he or she will be better able to help you. Don't exaggerate. If it turns out later that you made up some parts of the incident, it will be harder for others to trust what you're saying and to accept what really did happen.

The following is based on a true story:

It's Always Right to Tell
"This will be a secret, just between us. Promise me that you won't tell anyone."

Christopher lay on his cot, listening to Troy's words. In the dark of the cabin he could barely see Troy's face. "Christopher? Promise me, okay?" Troy was a college student. This was his first year as a camp counselor.

"Yeah, I promise," Christopher said quietly. They were whispering, so as not to wake the other boys in the cabin. Christopher wasn't sure why he didn't want to wake them. Maybe it was because he felt embarrassed.

"Good. You're a great kid. Get some sleep." Troy slid off the cot and went back to his own bed.

Christopher wasn't able to sleep. A short while ago he had woken up and found Troy in his cot, lying next to him. Troy was hugging him, and Christopher was confused, wondering if something was wrong. All the boys liked Troy. He was friendly and funny, a good athlete. Christopher had felt lucky to have him for a counselor. So he was shocked when Troy's hands began to touch his penis. Christopher felt his whole body tense up, and he found himself unable to move. He just kept hoping Troy would stop.

The next day Christopher avoided Troy as much as possible. Late that afternoon Troy left for his day off. Christopher gave a sigh of relief that Troy wouldn't be sleeping in their cabin that night. But he knew Troy would be back the next day. So Christopher gathered his courage and went to the camp director and told him what had happened.

The director listened to Christopher's story. Christopher was careful to tell everything that happened, in the order it happened. Some of it was embarrassing, and he found himself blushing. The director thanked Christopher for stepping forward. He immediately called Christopher's parents.

When Troy arrived back at camp the next day, the director confronted him with Christopher's accusations. Troy started crying and admitted what he had done. The police were called, and Christopher repeated his story for them. The detective was very nice, and he told Christopher he had done the right thing. If Christopher had not spoken up, Troy probably would have continued his behavior, and it would have gotten worse. Troy might have tried this kind of unwanted touching with other boys at the camp as well.

The boys at camp and their parents were told the truth

about why Troy was leaving the camp, and Christopher was treated as a hero for the courage he had shown.

Christopher was right to tell the truth about Troy's behavior. It is always right to tell. He found an adult he trusted and told him the whole truth from start to finish. Even though it was hard to do and a little embarrassing, he did it anyway. It was also good that Christopher spoke up right away. Ignoring this type of problem or hoping that Troy would just stop is not a solution. Telling an adult is the best way to get this kind of behavior to end. If the camp director had not believed Christopher, he should have continued to tell other adults until someone believed him and was willing to help.

When people care for you, it is hard for them to hear that you've been hurt, either emotionally or physically. It is normal for adults to want to deny what you're saying, because the truth is painful for them, too. They may feel guilty that they weren't there to help you. You may need to keep repeating what you know to be the truth until they really listen to you.

If you have been, or are being, abused (this includes physical abuse, such as being beaten or hit, or sexual abuse, such as someone touching your private parts or asking you to touch his or her private parts), it is important that you tell an adult you trust. Keeping the abuse a secret will hurt you more. Once you tell someone, that person can help stop the abuse and make sure you get whatever help you need.

If an adult says to you something like "Don't tell anyone; this will be our secret" or if you feel threatened or confused, it's okay to pretend to promise someone that you will keep the secret. But as soon as you're away from that person, *tell!* Most of the time, if you promise to keep a secret, you should keep that promise. But when someone is hurting you, or touching you in a way that you don't like, or abusing you, it is okay to break that promise in order to stay safe.

If you are confused, tell someone. Keeping this behavior a secret makes it easier for the person to continue to hurt you. Most likely this person knows what he or she is doing is wrong and wants to keep it a secret so as not to be caught. But it is much more important for you to stay safe than to keep your promise or to worry about someone else getting into trouble.

ANSWERS TO "WHAT IF...?"

What if . . . someone says that he or she wants to take photographs of you for a magazine or a modeling agency but that you can't tell your parents?

The fact that you cannot tell your parents should be a warning that this is not a legitimate magazine or modeling agency. Any legitimate business would want (and in most states would need) a release form from a parent for you to do any posing or modeling. Remember, if adults or older teenagers want you to keep something secret from your parents, you can be almost positive that they are doing something wrong. Tell a parent who these people are and what they want. They should probably be reported to the police.

Another warning sign would be a request that you go somewhere private and alone, like the person's office or home.

What if . . . your older brother's friend offers you a hundred dollars to deliver an envelope but makes you promise not to tell anyone?

Just say no. Walk away. Then tell someone immediately. You probably have a funny feeling already and know something is wrong. It's too good to be true.

The chance to make "easy" money can be very tempting. But if you are expected to do something dangerous or illegal, or if you get a funny feeling, it is not worth the risk. Check with your parents to see if they think the job or offer of money is legitimate. Tell the person making the offer that you need to check first with your parents.

What if . . . you think a neighbor is watching you through your bedroom window while you get undressed at night?

First, close your shades and make sure you can't see through them at night. If your shades do not conceal you at night, then undress in another room or ask your parents to get thicker shades or curtains.

Second, tell your parents. This is not a problem that you can handle alone. Even if you think you have solved the problem by closing your shades, the person may still be watching you. Ignoring it won't make it go away, so get some help.

STRANGERS

8

WHAT IF...?

What if . . . a homeless person approaches you and asks for money?

What if . . . you're hiking with your older sister and she twists an ankle. As she is limping home alongside you, a stranger offers to take you both to the hospital.

What if . . . you are riding your bicycle in a park, put it down to use the rest room, and when you return you find it's gone. As you are going to call your parents, a man approaches you and says he saw the kids who took the bicycle and could take you where they went.

We're all told to be cautious with strangers. This is good advice. But we don't always listen to it, especially if the stranger seems nice or you don't want to be rude. Unfortunately you can't tell good strangers from bad strangers just by looking at them. This chapter will advise you on how to deal with *all* strangers, no matter who they are, what they look like, or how nice they seem to be.

How to Identify a Stranger

You know not to talk to strangers and not to get in a car with a stranger, but who exactly is a stranger? Very simply, a stranger is *anyone you don't know.* This includes the nicely dressed woman who says she is a friend of your mother's, the teenage boy who delivers your evening newspaper, and the elderly woman shopping at the grocery store.

Most strangers are nice people. But some aren't. And you shouldn't have to try to figure out who's nice and who's not. Even adults can't always tell the difference. If you guess wrong, the results could be very scary.

There are people in this world who prey particularly on children. Some of them may have been abused when they were children, and that may explain why they grew up to be mean and abusive themselves. But it does not excuse their behavior, and it does not mean *you* should have to be a victim of their behavior.

Four Key Safety Rules

1. Keep your distance.

Remember that in Chapter Two we talked about keeping people you don't know or trust at least two arm's lengths away. Be aware of how close a stranger is to you. Notice if that person moves closer, especially if you've already asked him or her to stay away or to move back. If you feel threatened, don't let a stranger into your safe zone, the space that is two arm's lengths around you. And *use your voice to yell!* Don't be afraid to make a scene, get loud, and draw attention to what is happening.

2. Don't talk to strangers.

You don't owe a stranger an answer. You don't owe a stranger the time of day. Many times an assailant will test you, to see how close you'll let him or her get or how scared you are of him or her. Part of this test might include talking to you, asking questions and seeing how you respond.

Do not give away any personal information to a stranger, like your name or address, your age, your school, the kind of car your parents drive—anything! Also remember that nodding or shaking your head in answer to someone's question is a way of talking to that person, so don't respond at all.

3. Don't take anything from a stranger.

In order to get close enough to strangers to take something from them, you'd have to get within two arm's lengths, and that breaks Rule No. 1, which says, "Keep your distance." Even if what a stranger is offering is something that belongs to you or something that you really want, don't take it.

Also, just because people know your name does not mean that they know you. They could have read it on a name tag or on your clothing or overheard someone else use it.

4. Don't go anywhere with a stranger.

Criminals have a lot of good tricks to get you to go somewhere with them or to get close to you. They may ask you to help them find a lost dog, or they'll pretend to be lost or in physical pain or look injured and ask for your assistance. This is a common trick to make people forget the basic safety rules. One infamous criminal tricked his victims by wearing a fake cast on his arm and asking women to help him carry his groceries.

If adults need help, they should seek it from other adults, not from you. Your first priority is your personal safety. If you do think that someone is in trouble, you can help by notifying other adults or by calling 911.

Let's look at four different scenarios to see how well you understand these rules. See how early you can figure out when one of the rules is about to be violated and how you would respond.

The first two stories are based on real situations that were reported to us.

Keep Your Distance

Sharon noticed the man as she got in line to buy her train ticket. This was her first trip on her own to visit her grandparents, and she was a little nervous. Sharon had the feeling that he was following her, although whenever she looked his way, he pretended to be looking at something else.

Sharon bought her ticket and went out to the platform to await her train. A moment later the man also came outside and began walking in her direction. She could feel the knot in her stomach as he got closer. As he casually walked past her, he said in a low voice, "You're very pretty." Sharon did not know what to do or say.

The man continued on to the newsstand and bought a paper. He started walking back toward Sharon, looking around to see if anyone was paying attention. Keeping his voice low so only Sharon could hear, he said, "Where are you headed? Maybe we could sit together." As he spoke, he continued to move toward her. Since he seemed so concerned that no one else overhear him, Sharon decided to make a scene.

"Stop, that's too close," Sharon said in a very loud voice. The other people on the platform were startled, and they all turned to look. "I don't know this man! I want him to leave me alone!" The man's eyes got big, his face flushed, and he began to mumble some apologies as he backed away. He glanced around and saw everyone looking at him. He quickly ducked inside the train station and disappeared.

Sharon's choice of how to respond is a good example of how to pay attention to the distance between you and a stranger and how to maintain a safe distance. Not only did this man get too close to Sharon, he was also talking to her. She felt a knot in her stomach for a good reason. The man seemed to be testing Sharon. He was trying to keep what he was doing hidden from the other people around them, another warning sign.

Sharon picked a very good strategy: making a scene to attract attention and help. In a public place this is ideal, because Sharon could keep a safe distance by drawing attention to this man's behavior and forcing him to walk away. She could have also walked back to the ticket booth and told an employee about the man's behavior. She could have asked a security guard for help. The most important thing to remember is to keep at least two arm's lengths between you and a stranger.

Don't Talk to Strangers

Ashley and her friend Midori grabbed the last outside table and sat down to drink their lemonade. They looked up from their drinks and saw a man walk up to their table. He smiled as he reached them.

"Hi. I was wondering, do either of you know where the nearest ATM machine is?"

"Well, I think—," Midori started to respond.

"No, we don't have ATM cards. We can't help you," Ashley said.

Midori glanced at her friend, wondering why she was being so rude.

"Oh. I'm surprised. I guess I thought you were older. How old are you?" The man seemed very friendly.

"We're eleven," Midori answered. Ashley gave her an I can't believe you said that! *look*.

"Really, eleven? I would have guessed maybe fourteen. My name's Randy. What's yours?" He held his hand out to shake Midori's hand.

Midori had begun to reach out to take his hand when Ashley stood up and pulled Midori back into the café.

You may be wondering why Ashley wouldn't help the man. The girls were in a public space and were not in any danger. The guy seemed really nice. Even in situations where you think you can help, *don't.* An adult should not be asking a child for help or directions. It is not up to you to figure out who really needs help and who is lying. Remember the safety rule: Don't talk to strangers. This rule may be hard to follow, because it is natural to want to be friendly and help people in need. Ashley understood that answering this guy's questions would be breaking the rule. If he was close enough to shake Midori's hand, he was too close! Going into the café was a great safety strategy.

If target denial hadn't worked, do you think Ashley could have used her voice to set a boundary? Randy might have left them both alone if Ashley told him in a clear, loud voice that they did not want to talk to him. She might also have told him that an older brother or sister or parent would be coming out any minute. He might not continue to hang around if he knew someone older would see him.

Don't Take Anything from a Stranger

Tara was on the bus headed for home. As the bus lurched to a halt at her stop, she flung her backpack over her shoulder and exited the bus. Several other people also exited and scattered in various directions. Tara took off at a fast walk and was nearly half a block away when suddenly she heard someone calling, "Tara! Tara!"

She turned around to see an older woman hurrying toward her. "I think this is yours," she said as she held up a notebook with the name TARA in big bold letters artfully decorating the cover. Tara had pulled the notebook out of her backpack on the bus to check on an assignment and apparently hadn't put it back in her pack. The woman was loaded down with several bags herself, and Tara did not feel any threat from her. But as she glanced around, she realized they were alone on the street.

"Yes, it is mine. Thank you so much," Tara said. "Why don't you just put it there on that bench and I'll come get it?"

The woman looked at Tara, puzzled. "It's not a problem. I'm going in this direction anyway," she said.

Tara hesitated. She didn't want to hurt the woman's feelings. "I don't know you. You're a stranger. Just leave the notebook on the bench, please," Tara finally said.

The woman stopped and was silent for a moment. Tara felt really bad, because it seemed as if the woman was insulted. The woman mumbled something about ungrateful children. Then she dropped the notebook on the ground and walked away in a huff.

What Tara did was hard. The easy solution was just to walk up to the person and take the notebook. Tara was pretty sure that the woman was harmless. But Tara decided that the best way to stay safe was to have the woman put the book down so that Tara could pick it up. If Tara had let the woman hand her the book, she would have been within two arm's lengths of this stranger.

Sometimes strangers who mean to harm you may try to bribe you—with an offer to ride in a cool car, a gift of something really special like a bike or jewelry, even things that belong to you. If anyone tries to bribe you (even with something you really want), you should say no, walk away, and tell a trusted adult what happened.

Don't Go Anywhere with a Stranger

"Excuse me, can you help me out?"

Larry looked up from his Game Boy. A man was standing in front of him. "Hi. I just moved in across the street"—the man pointed to a light blue house partway down the block—"and I seem to have locked myself out. The bathroom window is open, but it's too small for me to fit through."

The man was a bit overweight, and Larry didn't think he'd be able to fit through any window in the house.

"Would you be willing to crawl in and unlock the front door? I'll give you five dollars for your trouble." The man pulled out his wallet and showed Larry the money.

Wow, Larry thought. Five dollars for something so simple?

"Sure, just let me ask my dad. He's right inside." Larry got up and turned toward his front door.

"Well, I'm kind of in a hurry. Can't you just come with me now? It will take only a couple of minutes. You'll be back before your dad even knows you're gone." The man looked at his watch as though every second wasted were precious.

"Really, it will only take a second. My dad's just inside watching the game." Larry had his hand on the doorknob. He knew he *had to get permission first, but he didn't want to lose out on the five dollars.*

What would you do if you were Larry? If someone offered you money, would it make it harder for you to say no? If the favor would take only a minute, would you be more likely to ignore the rules for strangers?

Did you notice these warning signs?

● A stranger was asking a child instead of another adult for help.

● A stranger was trying to get Larry to go somewhere with a bribe. The bribe sounded too good to be true.

● A stranger wanted this to be a secret. He did not want Larry's dad to know.

● A stranger was trying to pressure Larry into making a quick decision instead of letting him think about it.

Larry noticed all the warning signs and understood the rules. It was a smart idea to get his dad's okay before going anywhere with a stranger.

The last of the four safety rules is perhaps the most important. *Never, ever, go anywhere with strangers or get into a car with strangers.* Even if:

● They really seem to be in an emergency.

● They say your name and know where you live.

● They say they were sent by someone you know. *This rule applies even if they demand or try to force you to go with them. DON'T!* (We'll discuss in the next chapter what to do in this situation.)

ANSWERS TO "WHAT IF...?"

What if . . . a homeless person approaches you and asks for money?

The first thing is to keep a safe distance, which means two arm's lengths from the person. You can use your voice to set a verbal boundary and say, "Stop. Don't come any closer. I don't have any money." Or, "I can't help you. Leave me alone." Even if you want to help, giving him or her money means you have to break the safety rules. If you are close enough to hand over money, the stranger is close enough to grab you. If you need to walk by the person, make sure you keep your distance. Use your peripheral vision to keep an eye on him or her. It is okay to look over your shoulder once or twice to make sure that the stranger is not following you.

What if . . . you're hiking with your older sister and she twists an ankle. As she is limping home alongside you, a stranger offers to take you both to the hospital.

Do not accept the ride. This person is a stranger, and that means that all the rules still apply, even though your sister is injured. Stay two arm's lengths away and ask him or her to call 911 for an ambulance. Do not continue to talk to this person. Never go anywhere with a stranger.

It is a good idea to have a plan in advance. Discuss with a parent what to do and how you should get help.

What if . . . you are riding your bicycle in a park, put it down to use the rest room, and when you return you find it's gone. As you are going to call your parents, a man approaches you and says he saw the kids who took the bicycle and could take you where they went.

The rule about not going anywhere with a stranger applies even if you've lost a bicycle. It's hard to tell if someone is really trying to help or trying to trick you. You must keep the man at a safe distance when he starts to talk to you. Call your parents or the police. Also, you could tell the man to call the police with a description of the kids. If he really wants to help, he will. Do not go with the man even to get back what belongs to you.

FIGHTING BACK

9

We hope the tips we've given you in this book will help you avoid situations where you might have to fight. Fighting is always a last option. It should be used only in extreme situations. An extreme situation is one in which your life is in danger because a bully is going to beat you up or because someone is forcing you to go with him or her against your will.

Learning how and when to fight is something you need to discuss with your parents. Unlike the way most fighting is portrayed on television and in the movies, violence is not clean. Films and television shows do not show realistic fighting or when it would be appropriate to fight, so it is sometimes hard to figure out when it is a good choice.

This chapter will attempt to help you learn how and when fighting is appropriate.

HOW TO RECOGNIZE WHEN YOU NEED TO FIGHT

We've been giving you a lot of advice on things to do to avoid being targeted as a victim. But how do you know when it's time to fight? And how do you fight, especially if the other person is older and bigger?

● If you have tried to set a boundary with someone who is not listening to you, you *may* have to fight.

● If you've told someone to stop or to go away or to leave you alone and that person is not stopping or leaving, you *may* have to fight.

● If someone blocks your way and won't let you get to a safe place, you *may* have to fight.

● If your gut is telling you something is wrong and you feel your adrenaline starting to pump, you *may* have to fight.

● If someone reaches out and grabs you and tries to take you somewhere, you *have a reason* to fight!

ONE LAST CHANCE . . .

We've been urging you to use your voice throughout this book. Here are some strategies you can use and ideas for things you might say as a last effort to avoid a fight:

● Try to talk the person out of hurting you by saying things like "Do you have a kid? What if someone scared your kid the way you're scaring me? Think how scared you were as a kid when someone tried to hurt you."

● You can lie: "My dad will be here any minute to pick me up"; "I see my friends; they're right over there."

● Be forceful and loud: *"Get away from me now! Leave! I said back off!"*

● If there are people near enough to hear you, you might try calling out the assailant's description: "This guy won't leave me alone! He's got brown hair and a beard; he's wearing blue jeans and a red sweatshirt; he has on white sneakers!"

OPTIMIZING YOUR SIZE

You may think that you don't stand a chance against an adult or anyone physically bigger than you. But have you ever tried to hold a cat that didn't want to be held? That cat is much smaller than you, yet it can usually get away if it wants to. There are ways you can use your size to your advantage:

● Look for places you can run to where a bigger person wouldn't fit: through bars or holes in fences, under cars.

● If you're feeling threatened, put your hands up in front of your face and chest. You can use your hands and arms to protect your head and body if an assailant tries to hit you.

● Chances are good that you can move more quickly than an adult. Dodge, squirm, change directions. Watch the movie *Big,* and take a cue from Tom Hanks's character during the basketball scene!

ACHIEVING YOUR GOAL

It is important for you to understand that if you need to fight because your life is in danger, your goal is to hurt the attacker so he or she lets go of you and to *run!* And while you're running, *yell!* The goal is not to look like Bruce Lee or Steven Seagal. The goal is to run to safety.

Target Areas

Let's start with the basics. Everyone (even a big, strong guy) has vulnerable parts of his or her body. These areas are called target areas. They could be soft tissue areas on the body, such as the eyes and the groin area, or really sensitive body parts, such as the shin or throat.

Natural Weapons

Each of us walks around with natural weapons. These are body parts that we can use to defend ourselves. Your voice, hands, and feet are natural weapons. You can use your voice to attract attention to your situation or to yell loudly

into an attacker's ear. You can use your hands by scratching or by placing your fingers together into the shape of a bird's beak. Wrap all four fingers around your thumb. With a quick, jabbing motion, strike with the ends of your fingers. You can hurt someone quickest if you scratch a target area like the eyes or strike the bird beak into someone's eyes or throat. Your feet can be used to kick or run.

Essentially you can be attacked in two different ways: from the front or from the rear.

If someone attacks you from the front (grabs your arms or your shoulders or grabs you by the hair), you can:

- Kick the assailant in the shins.
- Kick the attacker, male or female, in the groin with your knee or the top of your foot (kick straight up between the legs).
- Strike the assailant's eyes or throat with the bird beak.

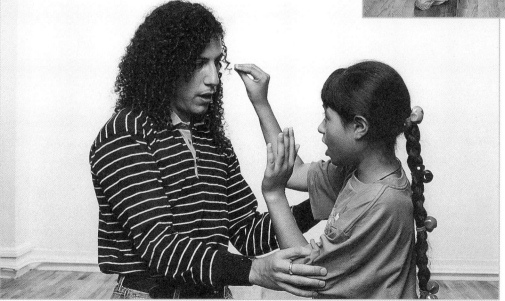

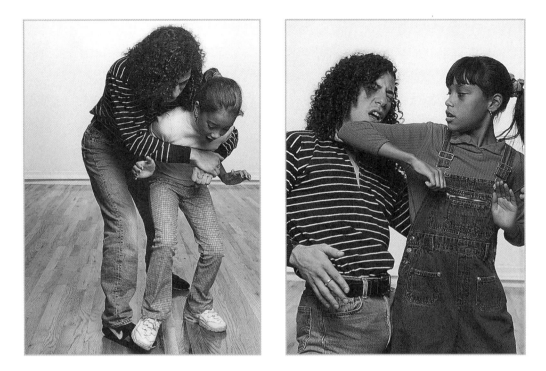

If you are grabbed from behind, you can:

● Scrape your foot down the attacker's shins.

● Stomp the top of the attacker's foot with your heel.

● Jab the assailant in the solar plexus (just below the rib cage and above the stomach), or the head or throat, with your elbow.

● Kick backwards with your heel, and aim for the groin or knees.

If someone picks you up, you can still use your legs to kick the person in the shins or the groin. If the attacker is holding you in such a way that your legs can't kick either target, see if you can reach the groin with one of your hands. Grab underneath, squeeze and twist, and don't let go!

Fighting Spirit

Fighting back in a life-threatening situation is really scary. It is hard (if not impossible) to learn these techniques from reading a book. The best way to learn any skill is to practice it over and over again. However, even if you have finely tuned skills, the most important aspect of fighting is spirit. Fighting spirit is about attitude and intention. If you have a lot of fighting spirit, you will look as if you mean it, as if every bone and muscle in your body were committed to fighting and were prepared to do whatever you have to do to win and get to safety quickly.

One of the best ways to get fighting spirit is to yell loudly with every strike. You can yell the strike ("Kick!") or you can just yell "No!" Yelling while you are fighting gets your adrenaline running through your body and makes your movements more powerful. It may also let someone else know you need help.

Here are some other tips:

● Don't forget about scratching and biting. They're always good options.

● Don't get into a long physical fight. As soon as your assailant lets go, *run!*

● If an assailant grabs one of your hands, use the other one. If he or she grabs both hands, use your legs.

● If you can, aim for the head and groin areas, because they are the most vulnerable.

Once you get the assailant to let go of you:

● *Run and yell!*

● Drop books, backpacks, groceries, or anything else you're carrying. They'll just get in your way.

● Make noise, or yell, "I'm a kid, I need help!" People are more likely to come to the aid of a child than an adult.

● Tell an adult what happened right away. The police can try to catch the assailant and, together with your parents, can make sure you are okay physically.

The following is based on a true story:

Fighting Back When You're in Danger
Stacy was talking to her friend Helen on a pay phone when she noticed a man walking across the deserted parking lot. Helen was supposed to meet Stacy at the record store, but Helen never showed up. Stacy had waited twenty minutes before deciding to call her friend. It turned out that Helen had forgotten about her aunt and uncle coming over for dinner, and her parents hadn't let her leave. Helen had tried to call Stacy and tell her, but Stacy had already left for the store. It was a huge mess.

So now Stacy was in a deserted parking lot. To make matters worse, there was a strange man walking toward her. He stopped a few feet away and waited. At first Stacy thought he wanted to use the phone. But then she got the clear feeling that he was waiting not for the phone but for her. She tried to keep her voice calm as she spoke to Helen; she wasn't sure if the man could hear what she was saying. "Helen, I'm in the parking lot by the record store, and I'm scared because a strange man is walk-ing toward me."

Helen said, "Hang up, and I'll call nine-one-one. If you can, call me back, and I'll stay on the phone with you till help comes."

Stacy hung up and headed back toward the street, where she had parked her bike. Her instincts told her to leave instead of waiting around to call Helen back. If she could make it to her bicycle or at least to the street, where there might be other people, she'd be all right.

"Where are you going?" the man said as he moved in front of her, blocking her way.

"I'm going home," Stacy said, and she tried to go around him. He took a step so he was again blocking her.

"I don't think so. You're coming with me." The man reached out and grabbed Stacy's arm. For a second Stacy froze. Then she got really mad. She kicked him hard in the shin, and as he bent over a little from the pain, she made a beak with her free hand and jabbed him—hard—in the eye. He let go of her arm, and she ran, yelling, "I need help!"

In this story Stacy was in a very frightening position: She was alone with a man who clearly meant her harm. But she did a lot of things that kept her safe.

First, she was aware of her surroundings. She listened to her gut and realized her level of danger.

Second, she told her friend that she was in trouble.

Third, she did not panic. She knew she could fight if she had to, and she fought back quickly and decisively. It is usually best to add the element of surprise to your attack. The man didn't expect her to fight back, and she used his surprise to her advantage. As soon as she could see that her techniques were working and he let go of her, she ran away.

WHAT IF THERE IS A WEAPON INVOLVED?

Most assaults do *not* involve weapons, despite what you may hear on the news. And when they are used, it's usually to scare you so you'll cooperate with the assailant.

● If someone has a weapon and asks you for a thing (your money, your backpack, your purse, your skateboard, your tennis shoes, your jewelry), give it to him or her. No thing is worth your life or your safety. Any of these things can be replaced. *You* can't.

● If someone has a weapon and wants *you*—wants you to go with him or her somewhere, or to get into a vehicle, or to go into a house or an alley or the woods—*run!* Do whatever you have to, and *run!* Do not get in the vehicle; do not go anywhere with that person. *Run!*

● If the assailant has a gun, make yourself a more difficult target by running in a zigzag and putting objects—such as trees, cars, pillars, or the corner of a building—between you and the assailant. The greater the distance you can put between yourself and the assailant, the harder it is for the attacker to shoot you.

● If the assailant has a knife, put as much distance between the two of you as possible. An attacker can't stab or cut you if he or she can't reach you!

● *Never get into a vehicle or go anywhere with a stranger!*

Conclusion

This book was written to help you understand more about your personal safety. We hope you will now be more aware of what is going on around you so that you can avoid certain problems entirely. That is the best self-defense you can learn.

It is unfortunate that television and movies lead us to believe that self-defense means fighting. Self-defense, as you've seen, has more to do with knowing and liking who you are. The better you feel about yourself, the less likely it is that you will ever be a victim of a crime or have to use the fighting skills we teach in this book. Good self-esteem means being able to set boundaries with people who make you uncomfortable—whether the boundary setting involves walking away from a classmate who is telling racist jokes or telling a relative to stop touching your body.

Trusting your gut and using your voice are the keys to maintaining safety. If something feels wrong, it *is* wrong. Anything that sounds too good to be true probably is too good to be true. Trusting yourself lets you respond to danger sooner. And the sooner you respond to danger, the more options you have for getting out of the situation safely. Unfortunately, most problems do not go away on their own. You need to solve them by taking some sort of action—whether it's walking away to avoid trouble or yelling for help.

Problems that you can't handle by yourself may be solved with the help of a trusted adult. Don't be embarrassed to ask a parent or teacher to help you in sticky situations. Believe it or not, most adults really do want to help. Remember, whenever anyone asks you to keep something a secret (touching, drugs, stealing—it doesn't matter what), you need to tell an adult. If that person does not believe you, then tell someone else. Keep trying until you find someone who will listen and who believes what you are saying.

Of course, a small part of self-defense is being willing and able to defend yourself physically, if you are in extreme danger. A good self-defense program will teach you simple physical techniques that are taught in realistic role-playing scenarios. Ask your parents or teachers where to find this kind of program in your area.

We have received dozens of success stories from our students, many of which you have just read. Read these stories again, and see if you can think of other personal safety strategies that we did not include. Think about possible scenarios and how you might get yourself to safety. The more prepared you are, the safer you will be.

ABOUT PREPARE AND IMPACT PERSONAL SAFETY

Prepare, Inc. (based in New York City) and IMPACT Personal Safety, Inc. (based in Los Angeles) are national organizations offering self-defense training to adults, teenagers, and children. Although we teach physical fighting skills in our classes, we consider fighting a last resort. Our main emphasis is on awareness, boundary setting, and verbal skills. We have learned from the graduates of our programs that these are the techniques they use most often in real life. These techniques can help you avoid situations where physical fighting might be necessary.

This book is a culmination of a combined twenty years of experience in the self-defense field. Both Prepare and IMPACT Personal Safety have been featured on numerous national and local television shows, including *Oprah,* the *Today* show, *Roseanne,* and *Designing Women.* IMPACT is a member of the Los Angeles Police Department Civilian Advisory Board on the use of force. Numerous schools throughout the country have adopted our programs as part of their curricula.

If you are interested in more information about our self-defense programs near you, call 800-345-KICK (5425).

GETTING HELP

FOR IMMEDIATE HELP: DIAL 911.

FOR HELP IN YOUR AREA:

Look up the following services in your phone book:

Salvation Army
This group sponsors a scouting troop program for boys and girls, which includes safety training. The Red Shield, a youth community center, is available in some cities and offers classes in martial arts. Its social services agency can provide referrals to local organizations in cases of abuse or domestic violence.

Volunteers of America
The organization offers drug education/prevention programs for kids. It provides emergency shelters for children in trouble as well as homeless shelters for families with children.

YMCA/YWCA
Programs vary from city to city, but most offer workshops in self-defense and martial arts.

Boys and Girls Clubs of America
Programs may vary, but many clubs offer workshops in self-defense and martial arts.

OTHER RESOURCES

Boys Town Crisis Hot Line
800-448-3000
Boys Town conducts research and offers programs to meet the needs of troubled children (boys and girls) and their families. Boys Town Press provides resources for youth-serving professionals, educators, and parents; call 800-BT-BOOKS. See Web site reference below.

Child Find of America
800-I-AM-LOST (800-426-5678)
This group offers assistance and referrals in cases of runaways or children who have been abducted as well as mediation for families where abduction has been threatened.

Covenant House Nine-Line
800-999-9999
This crisis intervention hot line deals with runaways, suicide prevention, and domestic violence. It offers referrals and can arrange conference calls to put a child in touch with immediate help.

Klaas Foundation for Children
P.O. Box 925
Sausalito, CA 94966
415-331-6867

415-331-5633 (fax)

E-mail: klaas@crl.com

Klaas works to stop crimes against children through awareness and proactive crime prevention. See Web site reference below.

Missing Children Help Center

800-872-5437

This nationwide hot line deals with runaways and children who have been abducted by parents or strangers. It works with law enforcement in finding children, and it offers referrals.

National Center for Missing and Exploited Children

800-843-5678

This organization offers assistance in English and Spanish. It assists parents and law enforcement in finding missing children and helping children who have been sexually exploited (abused by someone other than a family member). It also offers referrals to other nonprofit groups.

National Child Abuse Hot Line/Childhelp USA

800-4-A-CHILD (800-422-4453)

This hot line offers crisis counseling, information, and referrals. Calls from children receive priority.

National Council on Child Abuse and Family Violence

800-222-2000

This national nonprofit organization serves as a resource center on family violence.

National Runaway Hot Line
800-621-4000
This hot line offers crisis counseling to runaways or those thinking about it. It makes referrals and can provide free Greyhound bus tickets home. It also serves as a center where runaways can leave messages for their family and can set up conference calls between runaways and family members.

Red Flag Green Flag Resources
P.O. Box 2984
Fargo, ND 58108-2984
800-627-3675
This publications division of the Rape and Abuse Crisis Center provides resource materials, including workbooks, coloring books, videos, and games. See Web site reference below.

On the Internet

Boys Town
http://www.ffbh.boystown.org
Web site provides a history of Boys Town as well as information on its services and programs.

Global Missing Children's Directory
http://www.gmcd.org

Web site was created to assist in the search for missing children. You can search the directory by several criteria, including a child's name, age, or sex. Search results are displayed as text or graphics.

IMPACT Personal Safety/Prepare
http://www.prepareinc.com
Web site provides information on the programs, a list of affiliates, class schedules, and success stories from graduates.

KlaasKids
http://klaaskids.inter.net/klaaskids
Web site offers safety and protection tips, plus information on sponsoring Child Safety Day events.

Red Flag Green Flag Resources
http://www.glness.com/rfgf
E-mail: %20rfgf@netcenter.net
Web site includes information on the services offered as well as an order form for materials.

Other Books You May Want to Read

Dolan, Edward F., Jr. *Child Abuse.* New York: Franklin Watts, 1980.

Gilbert, Sara. *Get Help: Solving the Problems in Your Life.* New York: Morrow Junior Books, 1989.

Girard, Linda Walvoord. *My Body Is Private.* Niles, Illinois: Albert Whitman, 1984.

————. *Who Is a Stranger and What Should I Do?* Niles, Illinois: Albert Whitman, 1985.

Haskins, Jim. *The Child Abuse Help Book.* New York: Thomas Y. Crowell, 1982.

Kyte, Kathy S. *Play It Safe: The Kids' Guide to Personal Safety and Crime Prevention.* New York: Knopf, 1983.

Madison, Arnold. *Don't Be a Victim: Protect Yourself and Your Belongings.* New York: Julian Messner, 1978.

Park, Angela. *Understanding Social Issues: Child Abuse.* New York: Aladdin Books, 1988.

Quiri, Patricia Ryon, and Suzanne Powell. *Stranger Danger.* New York: Julian Messner, 1985.

Terkel, Susan Neiburg, and Janice E. Rench. *Feeling Safe, Feeling Strong: How to Avoid Sexual Abuse and What to Do if It Happens to You.* Minneapolis: Lerner Publications, 1984.